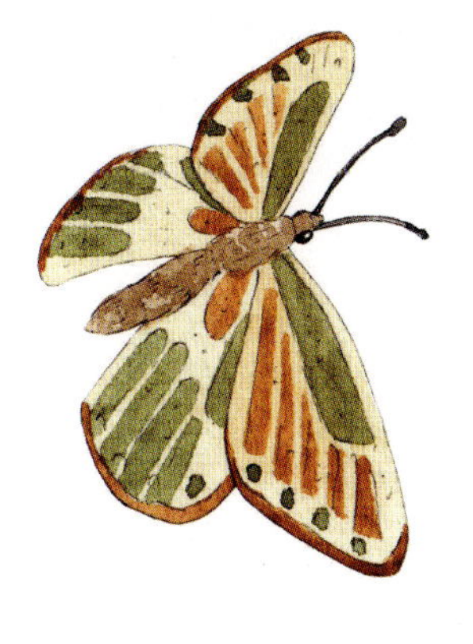
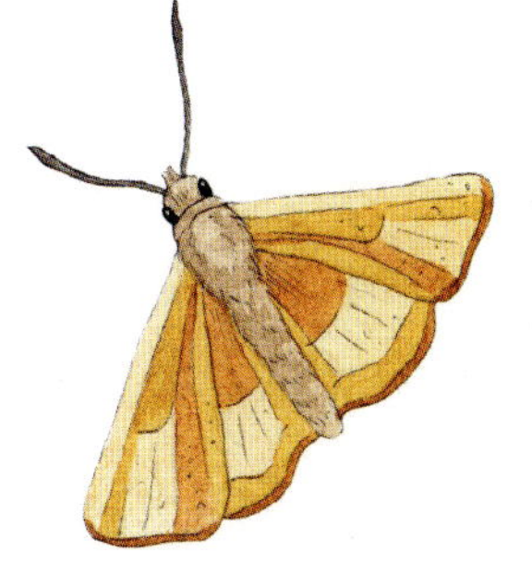
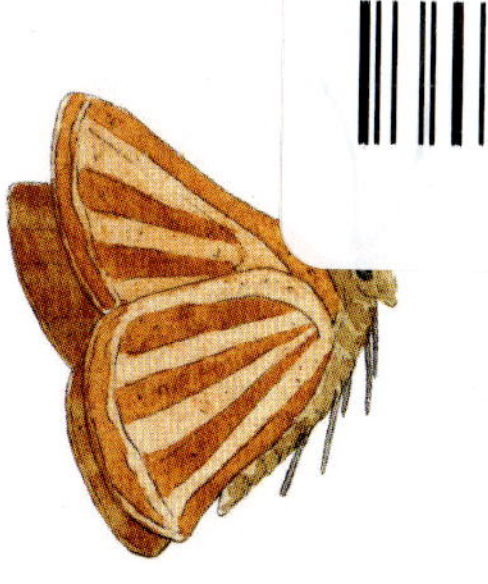

Boost Your
WATERCOLOUR
CONFIDENCE

OVER 60 EXERCISES TO BUILD SKILLS AND IGNITE CREATIVITY

KATIE PUTT

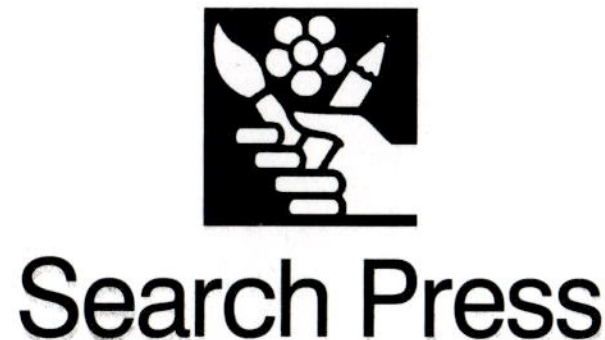

Search Press

Published in 2021 by Search Press Ltd.
Wellwood, North Farm Road
Tunbridge Wells
Kent TN2 3DR

This book is produced by
The Bright Press, an imprint of the Quarto Group,
The Old Brewery, 6 Blundell Street,
London N7 9BH, United Kingdom.
T (0)20 7700 6700
www.QuartoKnows.com

ISBN: 978-1-78221-933-0

Publisher: James Evans
Editorial Director: Isheeta Mustafi
Art Director: Katherine Radcliffe
Managing Editor: Jacqui Sayers
Editor: Emily Angus
Design: Anna Gatt

Printed and bound in China

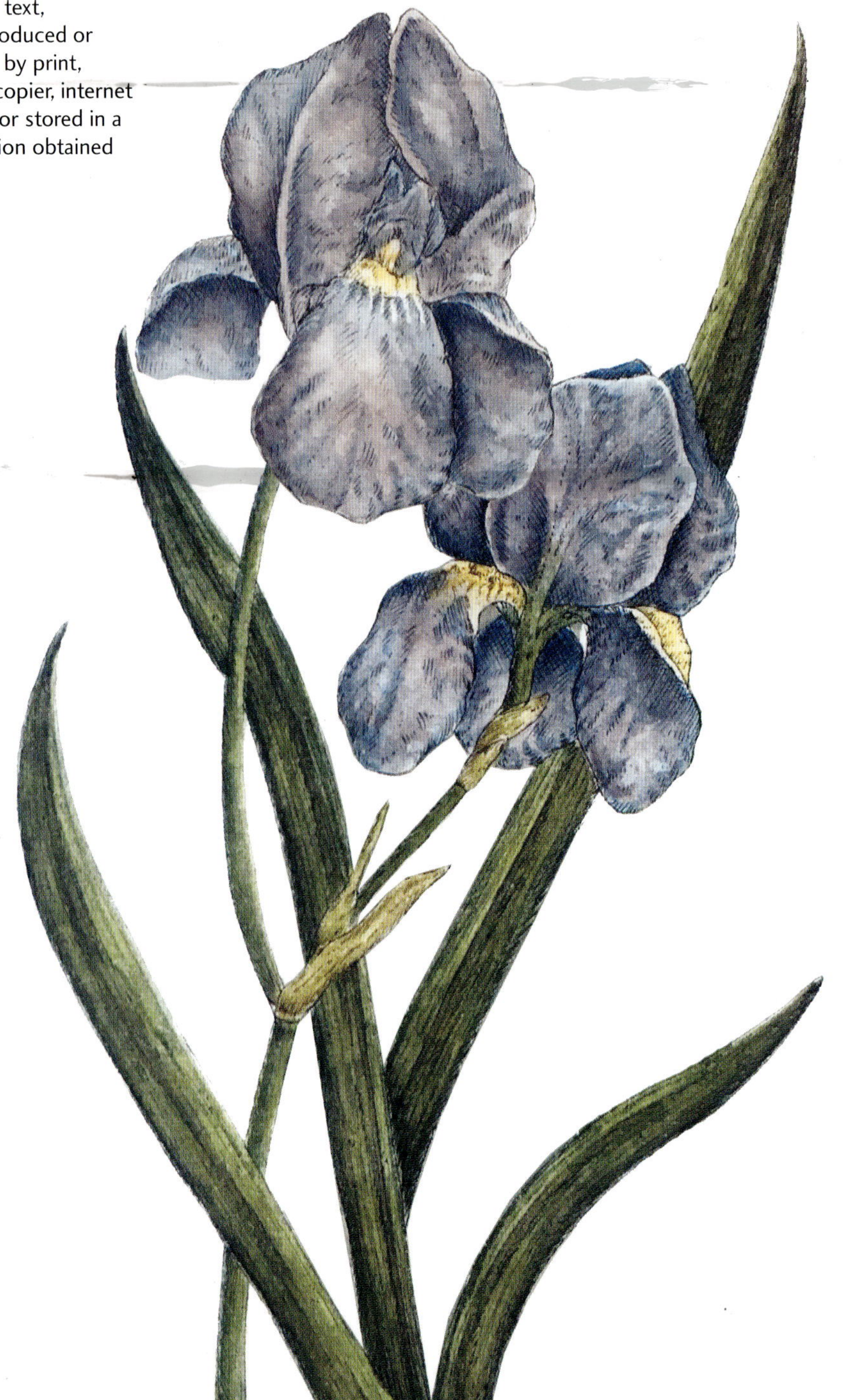

CONTENTS

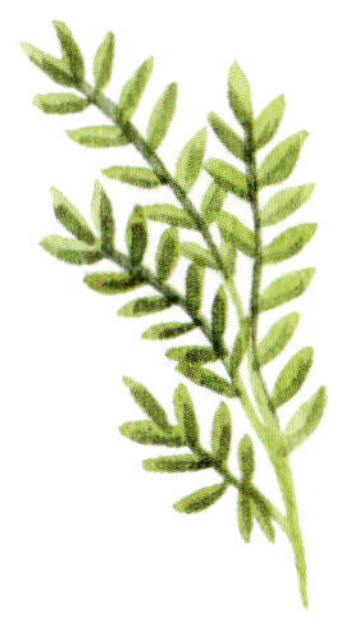
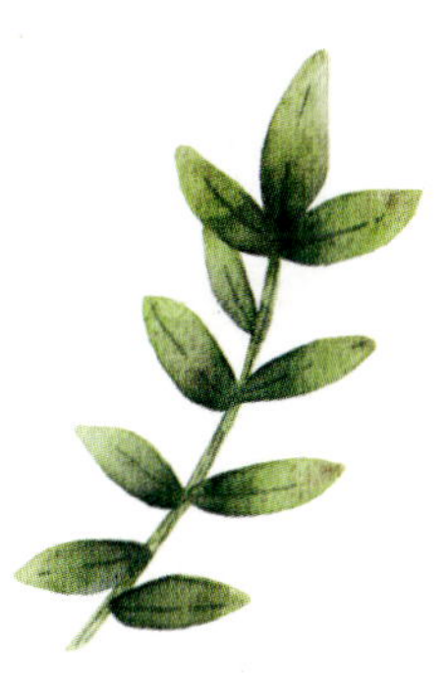

TEMPLATES

A gallery of drawings by the author for you to fill with colour, using the techniques from the first part of the book.

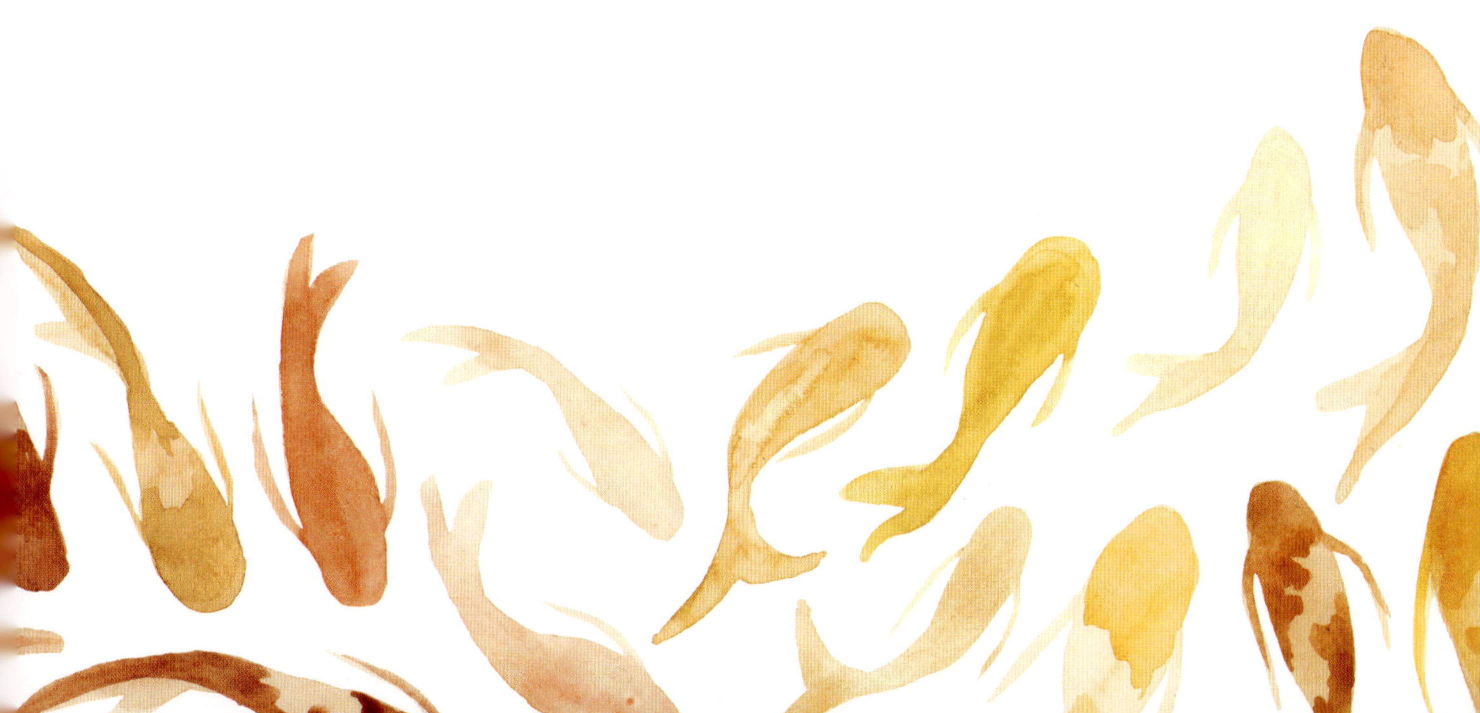

INTRODUCTION

Newcomers to watercolour painting often find the medium intimidating, because it can be tricky to control, moves as it pleases and behaves unexpectedly. But in many ways, this is what makes watercolour so versatile. After a while, and with a little practice, you'll soon find that it can be fun to let the paint flow and to see where it takes you.

In this book you'll find simple instruction on all the basic watercolour techniques, from colour mixing and basic brushstrokes to painting plants, foodstuffs and animals. As you progress through the pages, you'll learn the fundamentals of painting wet-on-dry and wet-on-wet, and you'll pick up tips and techniques for building colour, painting texture and creating the perfect composition. Complete with a collection of templates for you to work on, the book will help you to learn to paint with confidence while developing a style of your own.

MATERIALS

Paints
It's easy to buy a huge watercolour set with a rainbow of paints that draw you in, but all you really need are red, blue and yellow. With these you should be able to mix up every colour you want. However, to make life simpler it's better to buy a travel-size watercolour set containing 12 colours.

Basic brushes
Size 1 pointed brush (for detail)
Size 3 pointed brush (for general use)
Size 10 flat brush (for large washes of colour)
Household sponge or sea sponge

Paper
Choose 300 gsm (140 lb) watercolour paper. For smooth paper go for 'hot pressed' and if you want something with texture, pick up 'cold pressed' or 'grained.'

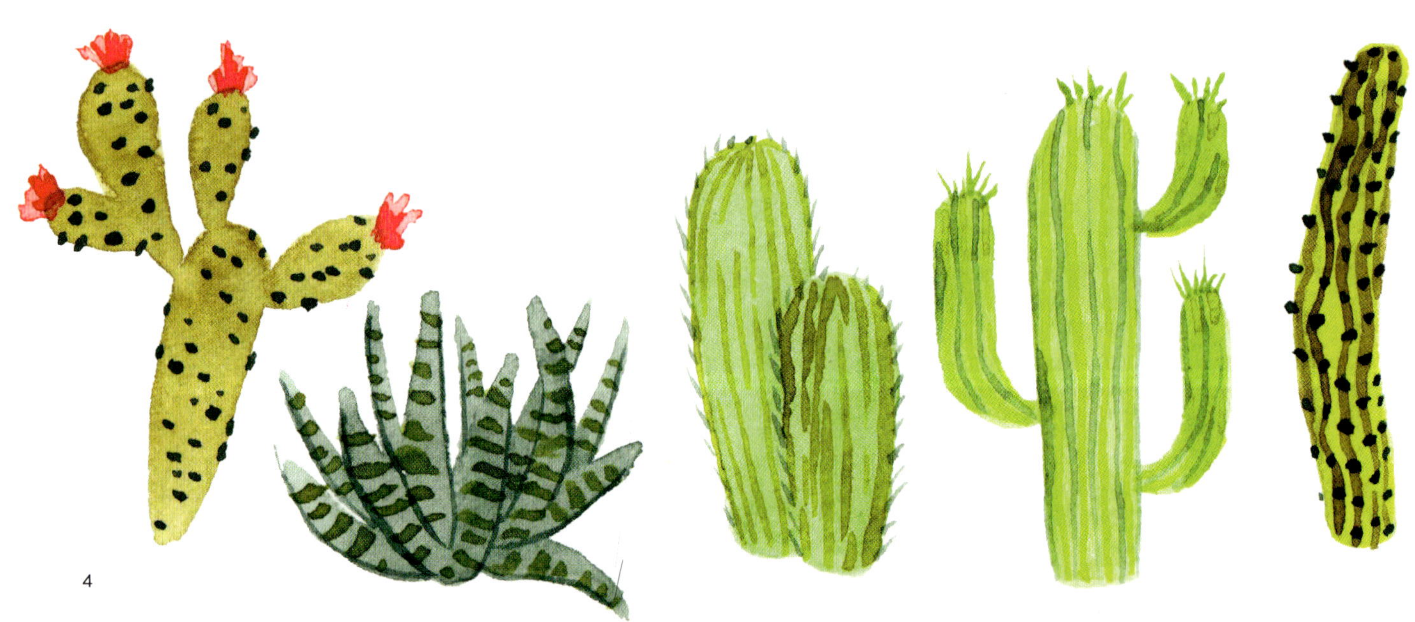

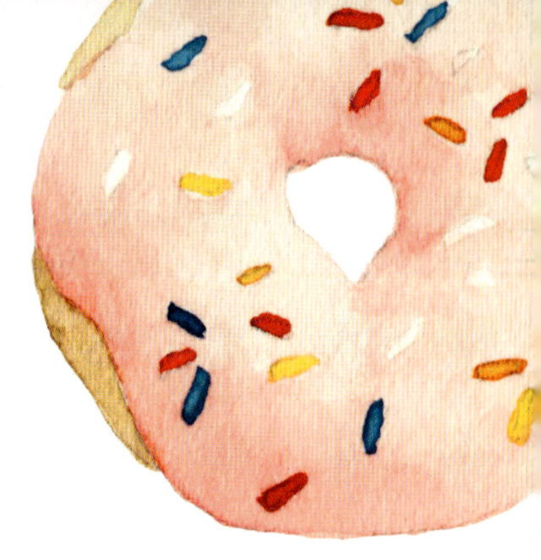

HOW TO USE THIS BOOK

GUIDED EXERCISES

The first half of this book (pages 6–47) offers over sixty exercises to guide you through a broad range of watercolour techniques. The activities gradually build in complexity, sometimes combining several techniques and showing how they can complement each other. If you find an activity that you particularly enjoy, repeat it using a different theme or subject. There's no need to rush through the book from start to finish.

TEMPLATES

The second part of this book features templates from a selection of the exercises in the first section. They are printed on special, thick paper, ideal for practising watercolour techniques. Some of the templates include images that are not shown on the exercise pages, allowing you to explore further using the same techniques.

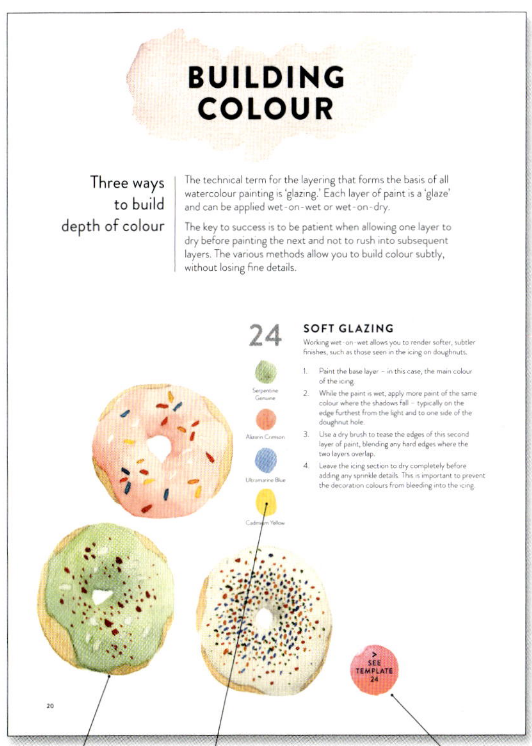

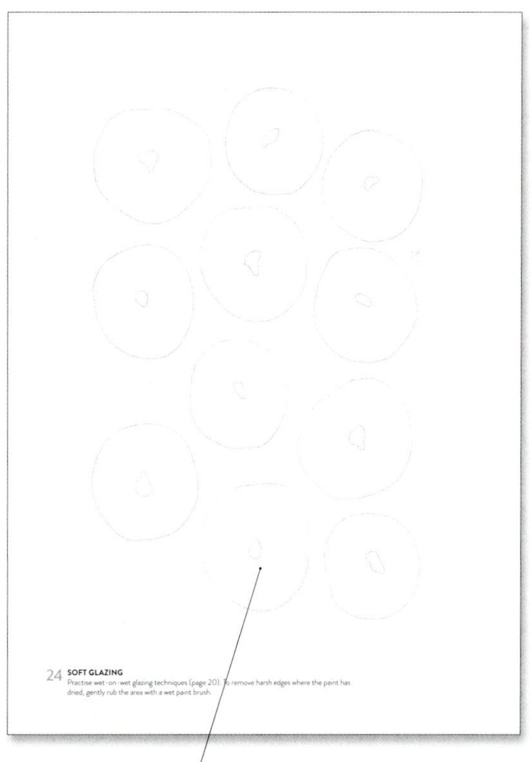

There is a finished painting alongside almost every exercise. This is an example of how your painting could look, but you don't have to copy it exactly.

Each exercise includes swatches of the paints used to create the painting shown. Use these to guide you when mixing your paints or experiment with your own choice of colours.

The circle indicates that the activity has a template at the back for you to try out the technique for yourself.

Each template has a faint outline for you to follow, a reminder of the technique you are practising and a quick tip for extra guidance.

UNDERSTANDING COLOUR

Three lessons on basic colour theory

A basic grasp of colour theory should underpin all your work, and there's no better way to understand colour than by mixing the paints you have in your set to see what happens. Push aside the fear of 'fresh' unspoiled paints touching on the palette and don't panic if your yellow turns blue, rather than the pale shade of green you were hoping for. Playing around with colour is fun. It will help you to find the right paint and water ratios while learning to make the colours you like and want to use.

1 THE COLOUR WHEEL

Having a colour wheel pinned up in the studio is incredibly helpful. You'll be amazed how often you refer to it. It is also very simple to create, as every colour is mixed using the three primaries: yellow, red and blue. Picture a circle on your page as a clockface. Wet your brush and paint a wedge of yellow radiating from the centre to the edge of the circle at 12 o'clock. Rinse the brush, and paint a red wedge at 4 o'clock. Repeat to paint a blue wedge at 8 o'clock. With the primary colours in place, you can start mixing. Try using different shapes, as below, to make your wheel more interesting.

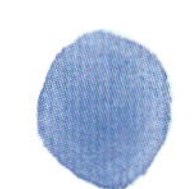

Cadmium Yellow

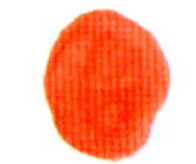

Ultramarine Blue

Pyrrol Crimson

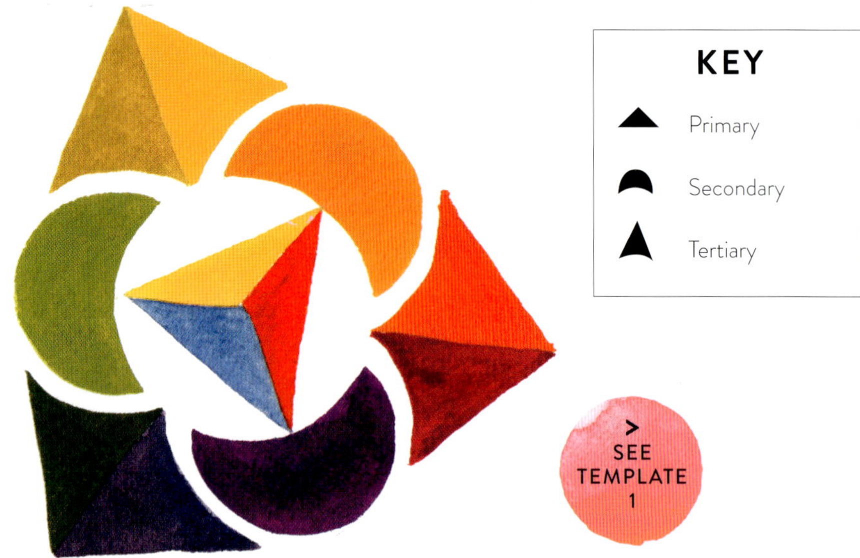

1. Using a palette, combine equal parts yellow and red to create a bright orange. Paint a wedge of this colour halfway between yellow and red on your wheel (2 o'clock). Repeat, mixing equal parts red and blue to create purple and blue and yellow to create green. Paint a wedge of each at 6 o'clock and 10 o'clock, respectively.

2. With the six secondary colours in place, you can mix the tertiary colours that lie between them. Work your way around the circle, mixing the orange you made in step 1 with yellow to make a light orange, and with red to make a dark orange. Paint in the wedges and move on. You will end up with a colour wheel comprising 12 colours.

3. You could continue working around the circle to make varying shades of each colour by manipulating the ratios of the paint you mix. But, for now, you have plenty of colours to work with.

Cadmium Yellow and
Ultramarine Blue

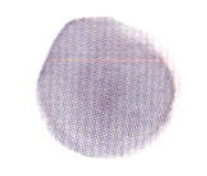

Cadmium Yellow

2 HARMONIOUS COLOURS

Colours that sit beside each other on the colour wheel are referred to as analogous or harmonious colours. They always work in harmony with one another. Work through the following steps to see this in practice.

1. Choose two colours on the colour wheel – green through to yellow, as here, purple through to blue, or orange through to red.

2. Wet your brush then pick up your first colour – in this case dark green – and paint a sprig of leaves. Paint the stem first and apply pressure as you pull the brush away from the stem to create each leaf.

3. Pick up the next colour on the wheel and repeat.

4. Continue until you have created a gradient effect with the leaf sprigs. If you were to keep working around the wheel, you would end up with a full rainbow of sprigs.

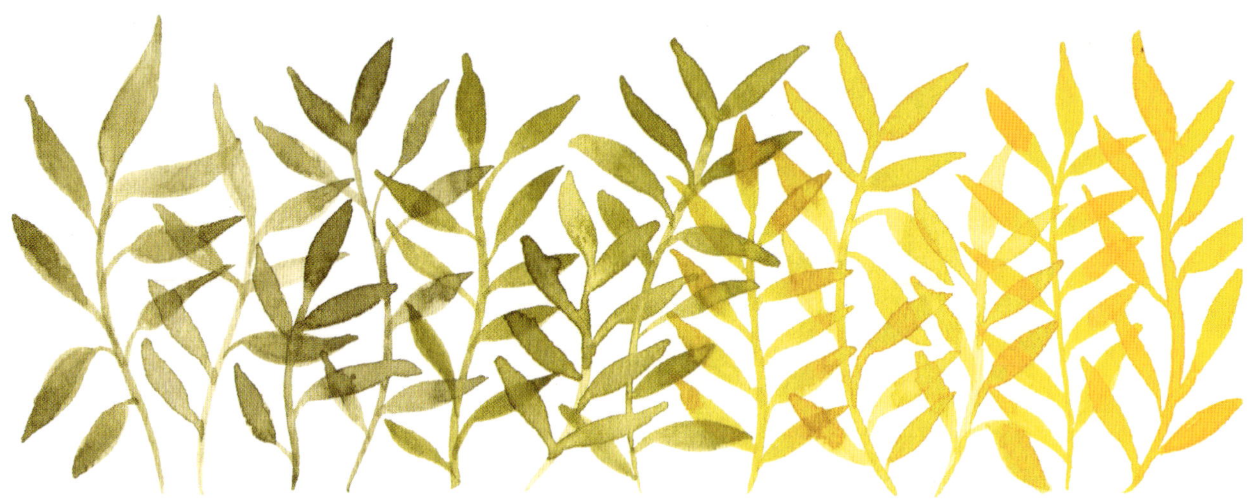

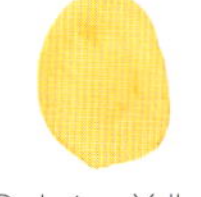

Ultramarine Blue and
Pyrrol Crimson

Cadmium Yellow

3 COMPLEMENTARY COLOURS

Complementary colours sit opposite each other on the wheel: yellow/purple, red/green, blue/orange and so on. Use them in combination with each other to make your paintings pop.

1. Pick two colours. The orange and purple shown here have a lovely Moroccan feel when used together.

2. Start by painting a swatch of the pure orange.

3. Add a small amount of the purple to the orange on your palette and paint a swatch of this new shade.

4. Again, add a small amount of purple to the now darker orange on your palette and paint a swatch.

5. Continue adding small amounts of purple to work through the various shades of orange, then brown, until you eventually arrive at a pure purple swatch.

6. You could use varying shades to create a mosaic that fills the entire page – you'll find the repetition becomes incredibly relaxing.

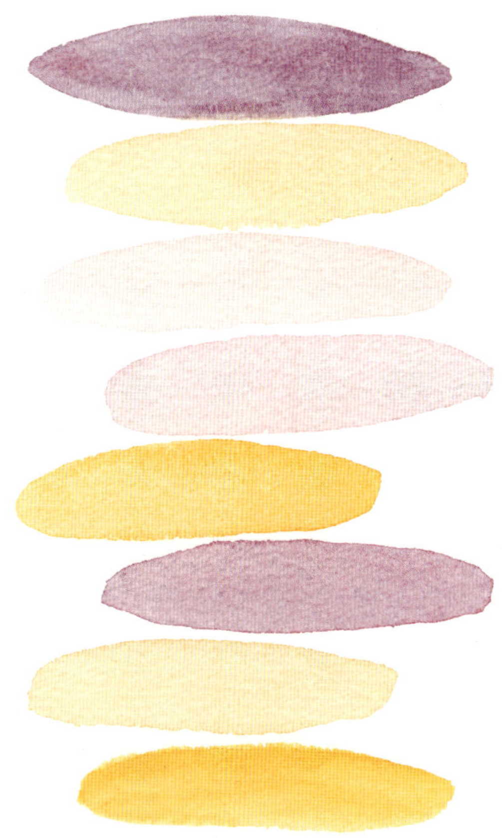

BRUSHSTROKE BASICS

Three key brushstrokes and an experiment

When it comes to using a paintbrush, there are many techniques to master and here are three to get you started. Not only are they the easiest to achieve, but practising them will make your strokes more refined in the long term. Practise until you find a way of holding the brush that feels comfortable.

4   STRAIGHT LINES

This simple movement can be very satisfying once you get into the zone.

Deep Ochre

1. Wet your brush, remove excess water, and pick up your paint.
2. Hold the brush in your hand in the same way that you would hold a pencil, and lightly touch the brush to the paper. Applying the same pressure throughout, slowly drag the brush across the page.
3. Repeat the movement over and over, using varying degrees of pressure. The lightest touch creates thin lines, whereas increased pressure widens the lines with more of the brush coming into contact with the paper.

5   WAVY LINES

This activity is similar to the one above, but sees you changing the pressure as you drag the brush. See the effect this has on the lines you paint.

1. Pick up some paint with your wet brush and hold the brush like a pencil.
2. Make contact with the paper, then increase and decrease the pressure of the brush as you drag it across the paper.
3. You'll find that you create a 'wavy', thin-thick-thin line. Continue experimenting and see what shapes you can create using this technique.

6   DAB AND PULL

This dab-and-pull method is a key technique (see also, pages 22–23). You can use it to create beautiful leaf shapes, animal markings and so on.

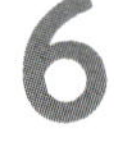

Cadmium Orange

1. Dab the paint onto the paper and, without losing contact, pull the brush downwards. Increase the pressure to widen the brushstroke.
2. Lift the brush off the paper leaving a petal shape.
3. To create a curved petal shape, rotate the brush slightly as you pull.
4. Create curves in the opposite direction by rotating the brush anticlockwise.

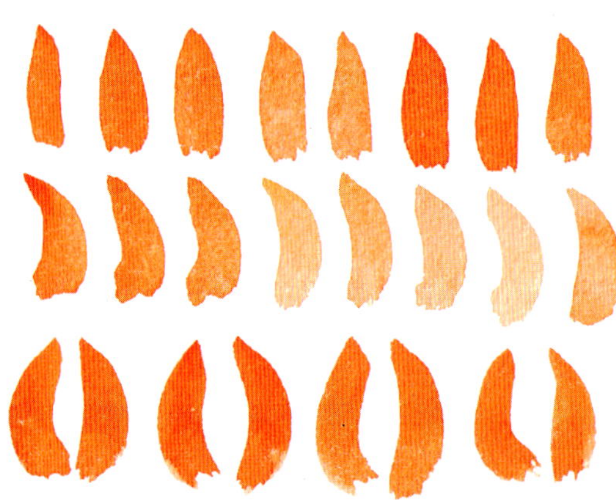

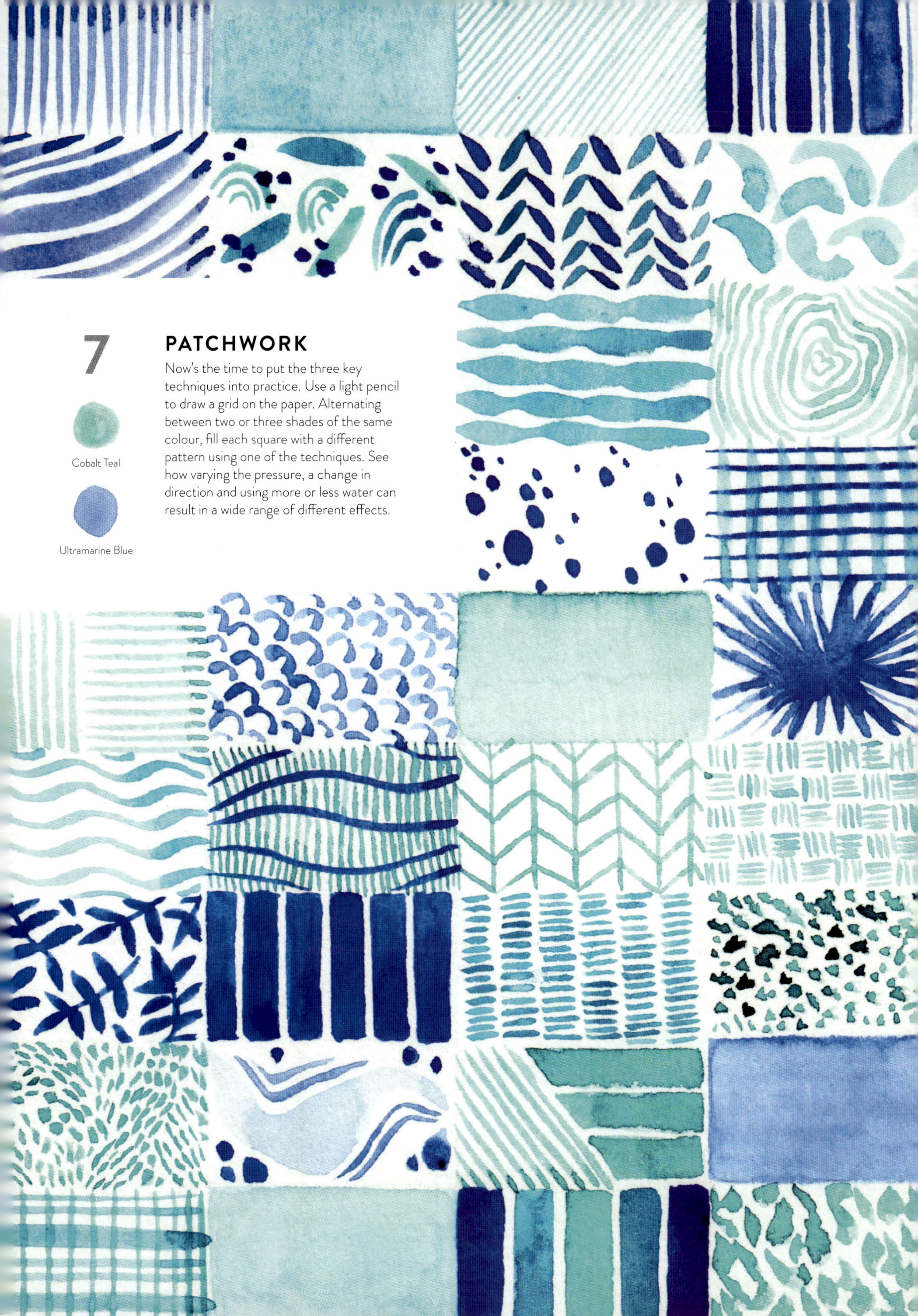

7

Cobalt Teal

Ultramarine Blue

PATCHWORK

Now's the time to put the three key techniques into practice. Use a light pencil to draw a grid on the paper. Alternating between two or three shades of the same colour, fill each square with a different pattern using one of the techniques. See how varying the pressure, a change in direction and using more or less water can result in a wide range of different effects.

DITCHING THE PENCIL

Three techniques for 'drawing' with the paintbrush

Pencil marks are visible through watercolours and cannot be rubbed away once the paint has locked them in. One way around this is to 'draw' with your paintbrush instead. In fact, going straight in with a paintbrush is often more expressive and can result in more life-like shapes. The following techniques will help you gain confidence, allowing you to trust your instincts in letting the paint express itself.

8 PATTERNS AND TEXTURES

With visible stitches and distinct patterns, knitwear is great for experimenting with texture.

1. With your wet brush, collect some of your chosen paint from your palette.
2. Using just the tip of the brush, make a series of small marks, gradually building them up to create the shape of a piece of clothing – a hat, a jumper or a scarf.
3. Experiment with a change in the direction of your marks to add movement, texture and more shape.

9 WORKING IN A SINGLE LAYER

Organic objects make good practice pieces, having irregular lines and diverse shapes. Vegetables don't have to be perfect; they even look better – and more realistic – when slightly wonky.

Deep Ochre

Alizarin Crimson

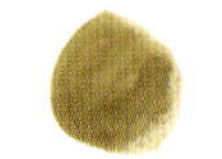

Cadmium Yellow and Ultramarine Blue

1. Fill your brush with paint and use the full brush to create an outline of a vegetable.
2. While the paint is still wet, fill in the centre of the shape. If you loaded your brush with a lot of paint at the start, you should be able to continue without having to go back to your palette for more.
3. Create just one layer of block colour without worrying too much if it is patchy in places. Leave the paint to dry.
4. Later, if there are any leaves or roots to add, paint them in the same way, in a single layer.

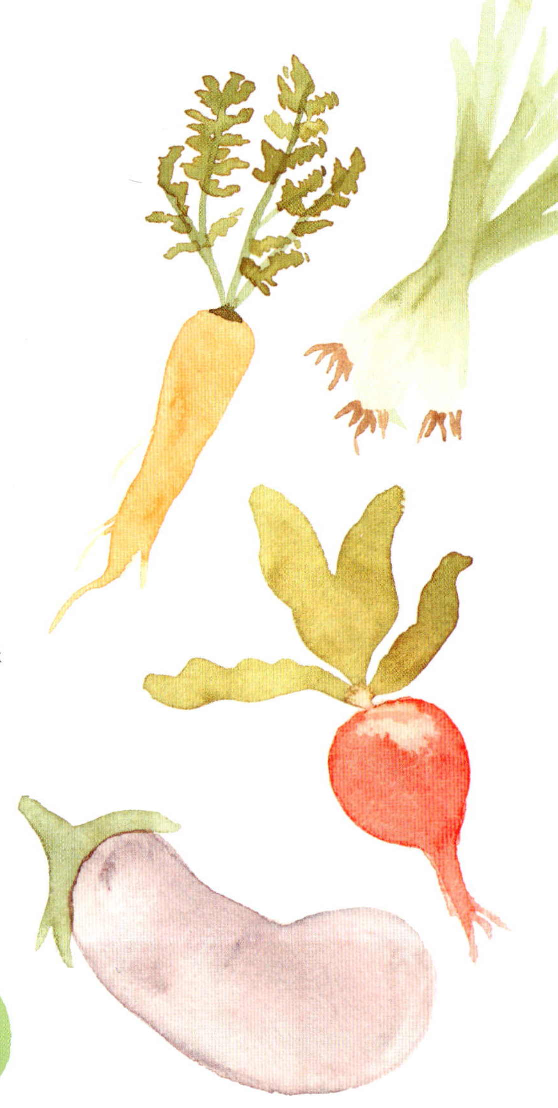

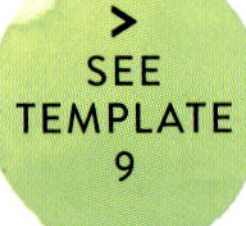

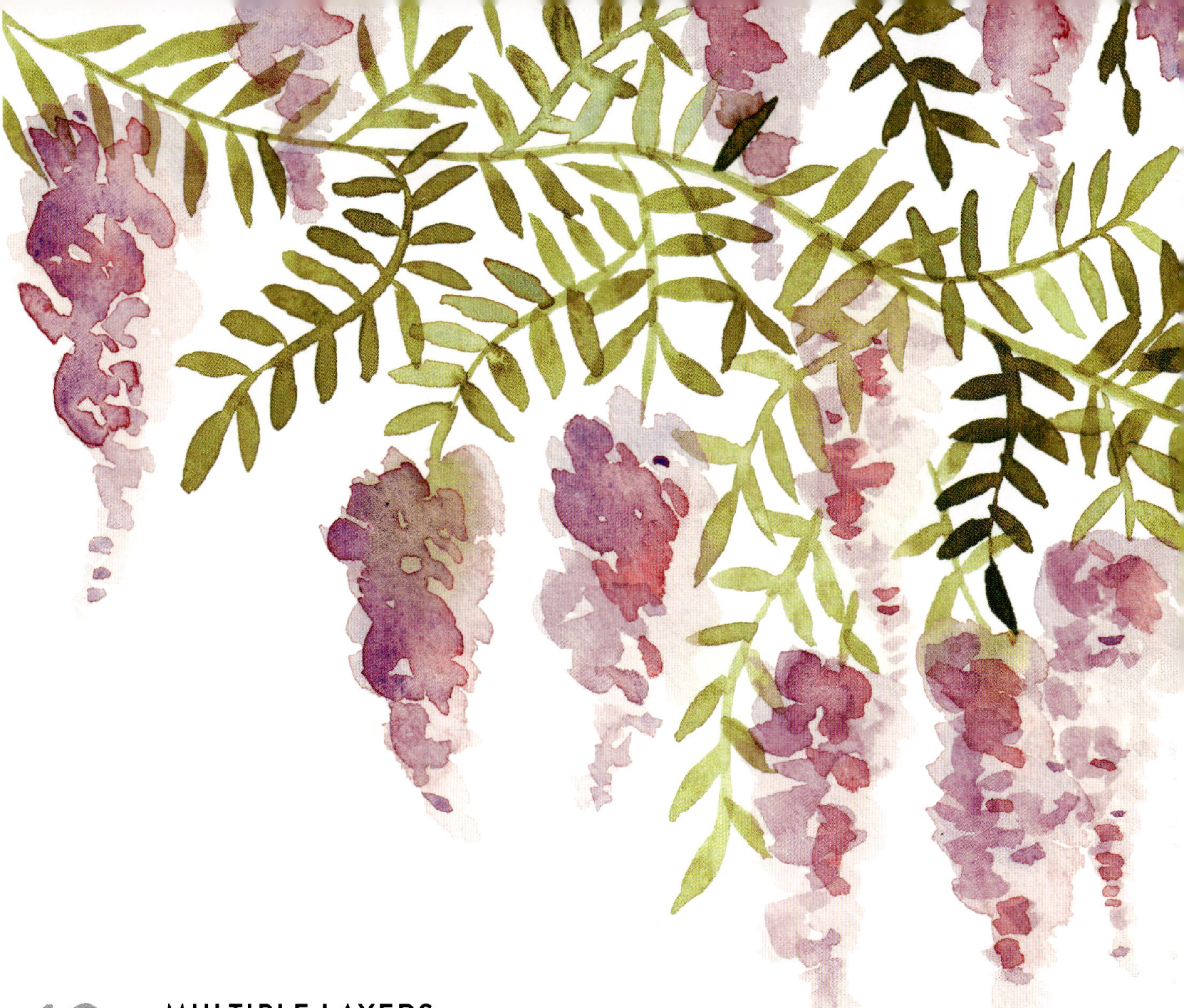

10   MULTIPLE LAYERS

This exercise demonstrates how you can 'draw' the delicate blossoms of a plant – in this case wisteria – using several layers to build colour. Besides the brushstroke basics on pages 8–9, it uses a new technique: dabbing.

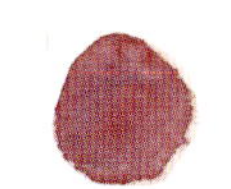

Ultramarine Blue and Pyrrol Crimson

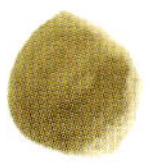

Cadmium Yellow and Ultramarine Blue

1. Collect some paint with a wet brush. Using just the tip, make contact with the paper and slowly drag the paint in a wavy line to create the shape of your branch.

2. Use the dab-and-pull technique to create the leaves. Place the tip of your brush on the branch. As you pull away, apply pressure to flatten the brush and widen the stroke. Gradually reduce the pressure again to complete each leaf using just the tip again.

3. Using a very dilute mix of the wisteria colour, create the basic shape of each blossom by dabbing the paint on to the page to form an inverted triangle. Leave spaces between some dabs, while allowing others to overlap.

4. With less water and more paint this time, but still dabbing, use the same colour to create shadows in the flowers, allowing patches of the paint beneath to show through.

5. Mix a brighter purple to create the final focal points. Again, use a dabbing action to apply the paint.

LESS IS MORE

The basis of working with watercolour is not to add white paint to make lighter shades of a colour, but to add water – the more water you add, the more transparent the paint becomes. Mixing white paint with a colour will not make it lighter; it will make it cloudy and opaque.

The most striking results can come from limiting colours or techniques in one painting. Some incredible monochrome pieces are created in this way. Like harmonious and complementary colour palettes (see page 7), a monochrome palette will always look appealing.

11 SINGLE COLOUR SHADES

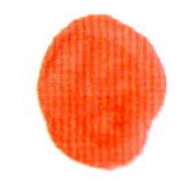

Pyrrol Crimson

You can create several shades of the same colour, simply by varying the amount of water you add to the pigment.

1. Start by getting your brush very wet and creating a little pool of water on the red on your palette.

2. Next, pick up a small amount of diluted red pigment and use this to create an apple shape on your paper with the brush.

3. Clean your brush and this time dip the brush for a while longer in the red to collect a little more pigment and make another apple.

4. Continue in this way, reducing the amount of water on the brush and increasing the amount of pigment you pick up, until you have a row of apples ranging in colour from a soft pink through to a bright red.

5. Once they have dried, add stalks and leaves to your apples in the same way, gradually reducing the water and increasing the pigment as you move from one to the next.

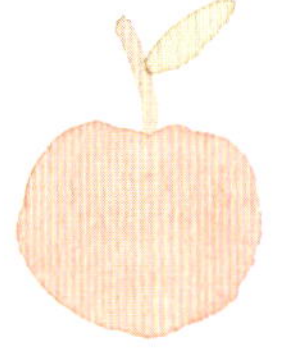 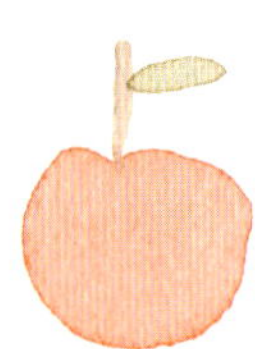 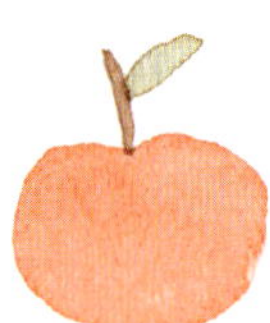 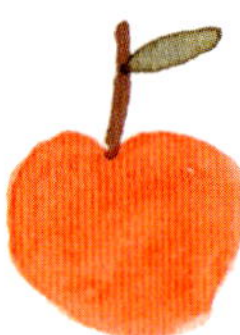 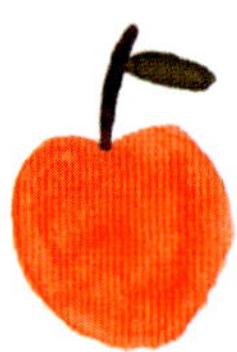

12 BUILDING WASHES

Ultramarine Blue and Pyrrol Crimson

Ultramarine Blue and Pyrrol Crimson

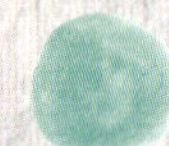

Cobalt Teal

Using the same process as above, you can create distance in a hilly landscape. Reduce the amount of water in a series of overlapping washes to create increasingly darker hills as you reach the foreground of your painting.

1. Using a pencil, lightly sketch the outline of your landscape. This might consist of four or five hilly ridges that sit above each other.

2. Choose one colour from your palette and create a little pool of water on that colour.

3. With a very wet brush, collect a small amount of pigment and paint the most distant hills in this shade.

4. Using a second colour, collect slightly more pigment and use this shade to fill a row of intermediate hills. See how you create more depth where the colours overlap.

5. Repeat step 4 to fill the next row of intermediate hills using a third colour, this time with even less water and more pigment.

6. Continue in this way until you have filled each section, with the darkest hills in the foreground.

13 LAYERING SINGLE COLOURS

Ultramarine Blue

Ultramarine Blue and
Pyrrol Crimson

Ultramarine Blue and
Pyrrol Crimson

This layering exercise demonstrates how you can use a single colour to create depth and three-dimensionality in a painting. It starts by using the single-layer technique described on page 10.

1. Create an outline of your subject – in this case a jellyfish – using a light wash of colour. But rather than filling the entire shape with colour, leave some areas unpainted. The white of the paper will show through to create highlights in the finished piece.

2. Once the first layer is dry, use a wash with a little less water and more pigment to paint over the outer edges of the jellyfish in a darker colour. Select the areas carefully, leaving some of the previous wash and the paper unpainted. You will have started to create depth.

3. Once the second paint layer is dry, add the finer details of the jellyfish using an even less-dilute wash. Use this darkest colour sparingly to add shadows to the jellyfish body and to add greater definition to its tentacles.

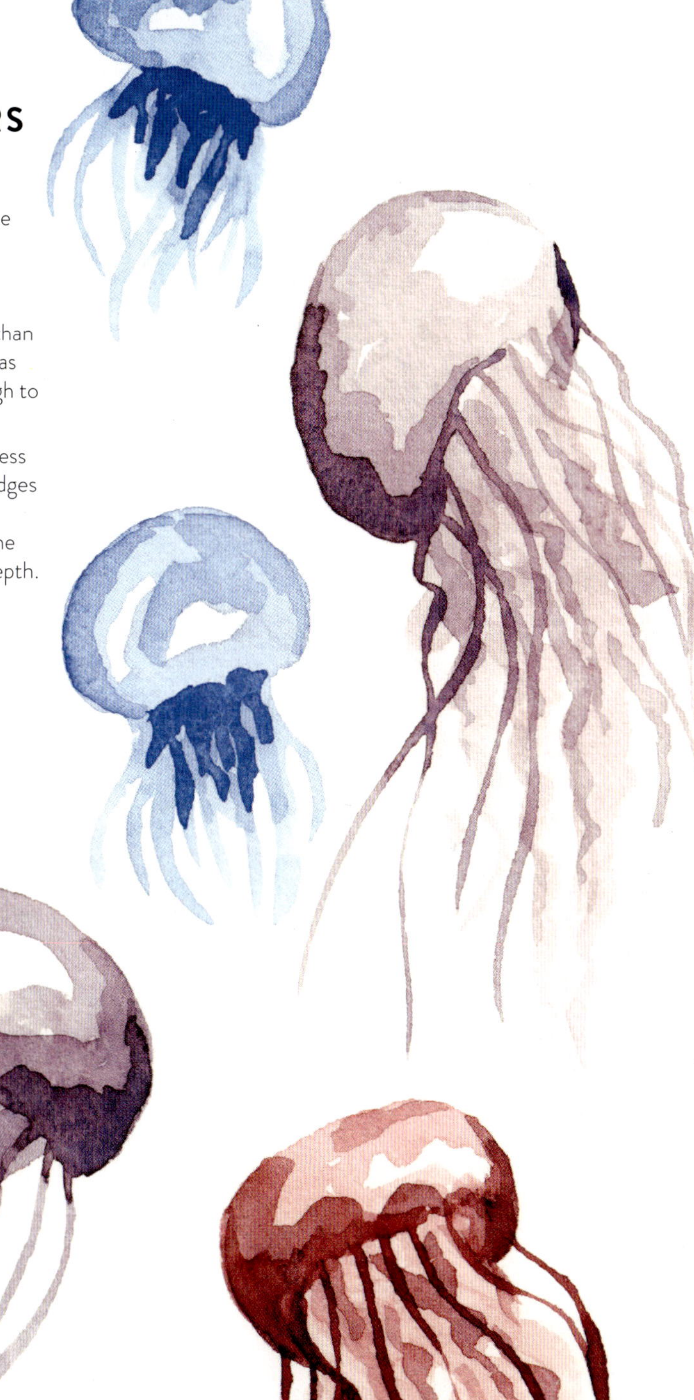

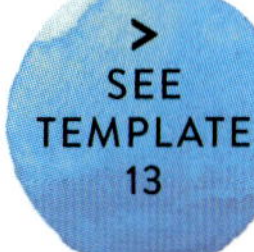

LETTING COLOURS BLEED

Three simple wet-on-wet experiments

A major feature of watercolour painting is that colours run if you don't let one layer dry before adding another; the paint will simply follow the route of the water and travel as far as it can. This can be maddening, but it can also be used to great effect.

In order to make the most of this in your own work, try these experiments painting wet-on-wet so that you know what to expect.

14   SIMPLE BLEEDING

Take any one colour and, with a very wet brush, paint several circles across the page. While each circle is still wet, paint a second circle slightly overlapping and watch the colours bleed into each other to create a marble effect.

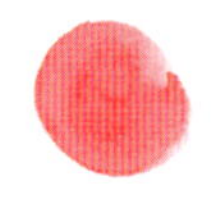

Pyrrol Crimson

Cadmium Yellow

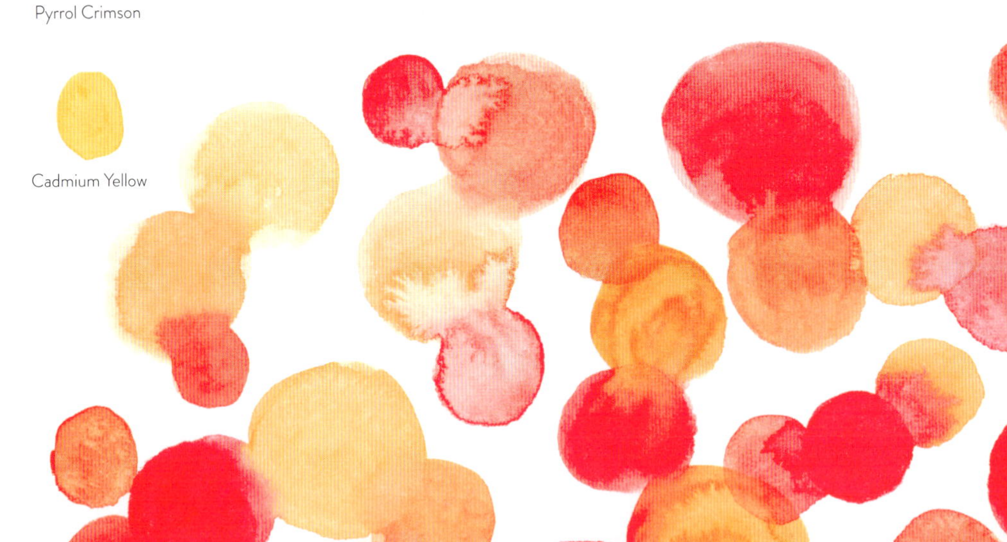

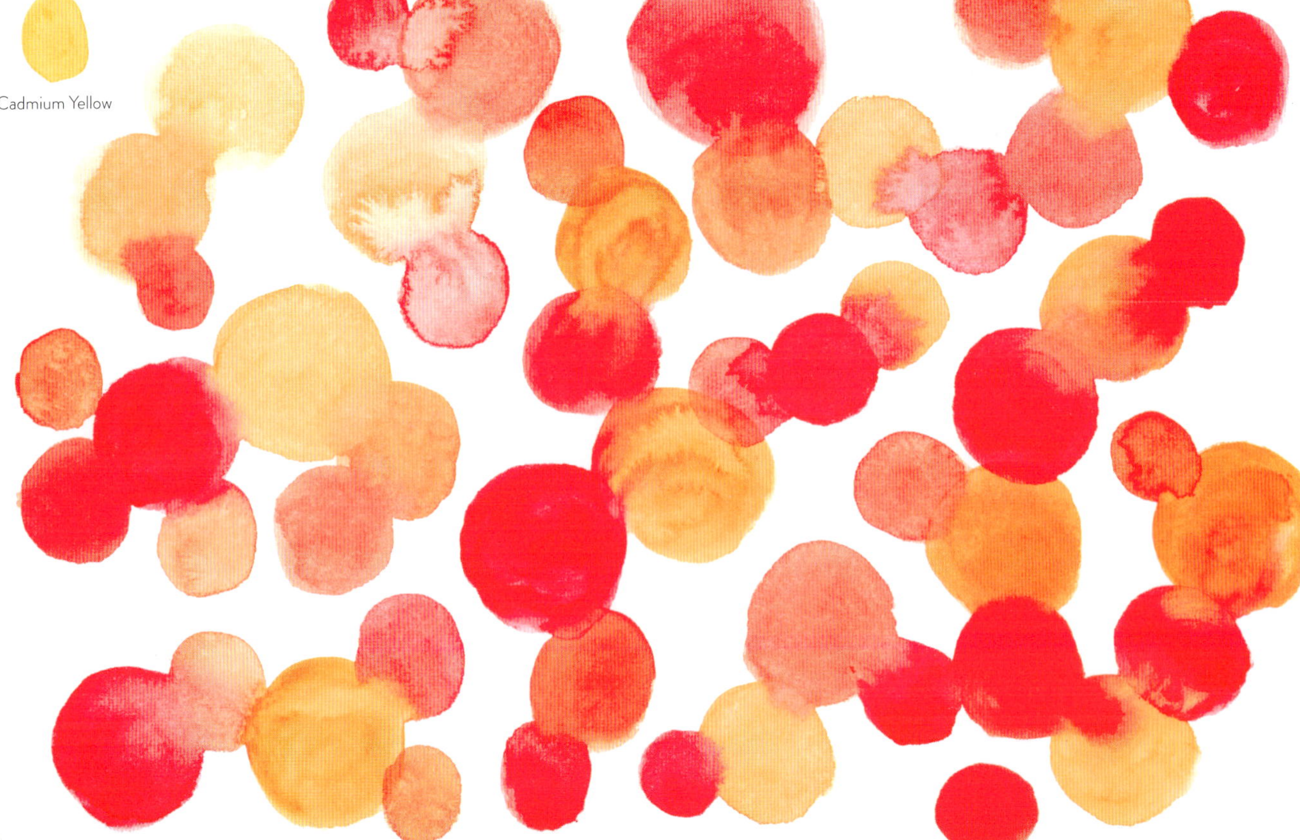

15 DELIBERATE BLEEDING

Rather than letting the paint move freely, see if you can control it. These watermelon wedges offer the perfect opportunity.

Cadmium Yellow

Green Gold

Pyrrol Crimson and Ultramarine Blue

1. Using a pencil, lightly draw the outline of your watermelon wedges – don't worry about the edges being too straight.

2. Create a watered-down red on your palette and use it to paint a watermelon wedge, stopping a little short of the rind area. As you work, take care to leave white spaces for highlights and to allow the paint to collect here and there. This will give the wedge texture. Keep the paint wet so you can blend it and avoid hard edges.

3. Using dark green, and staying well clear of the red, paint the outer edge of the wedge to create the rind.

4. Mix dark green with yellow to create a vibrant light green. While the rind is still wet, paint alongside the dark green allowing the colours to bleed slightly, but make sure there is still a gap between this light green and the red.

5. Water down the light green even more and dab the brush here and there along the white space, leaving it to blend slowly into the red.

6. Leave the watermelon wedge to dry completely before adding small dashes of black paint for the seeds. Use just the tip of a fine brush.

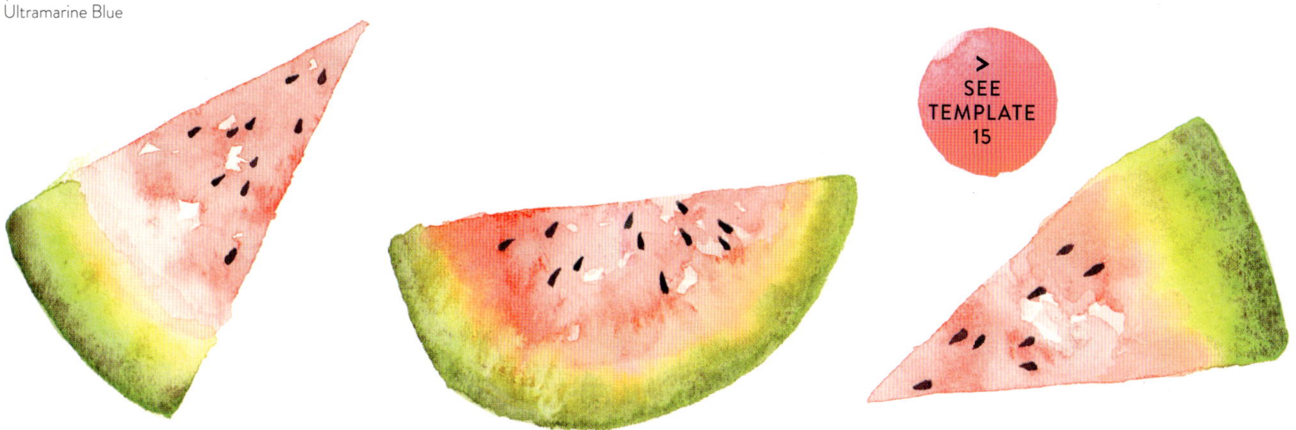

> SEE TEMPLATE 15

16 EXPERIMENTAL BLEEDING

Have fun and experiment with controlling the paint as it bleeds, as well as allowing it to spread freely. Create an abstract piece by loading a large, flat brush with plenty of water. As you apply different colours, leave them to bleed into your previous brushstrokes here and there. Let your hand move freely and see what you can create.

Cadmium Yellow

Green Gold

Pyrrol Crimson and Ultramarine Blue

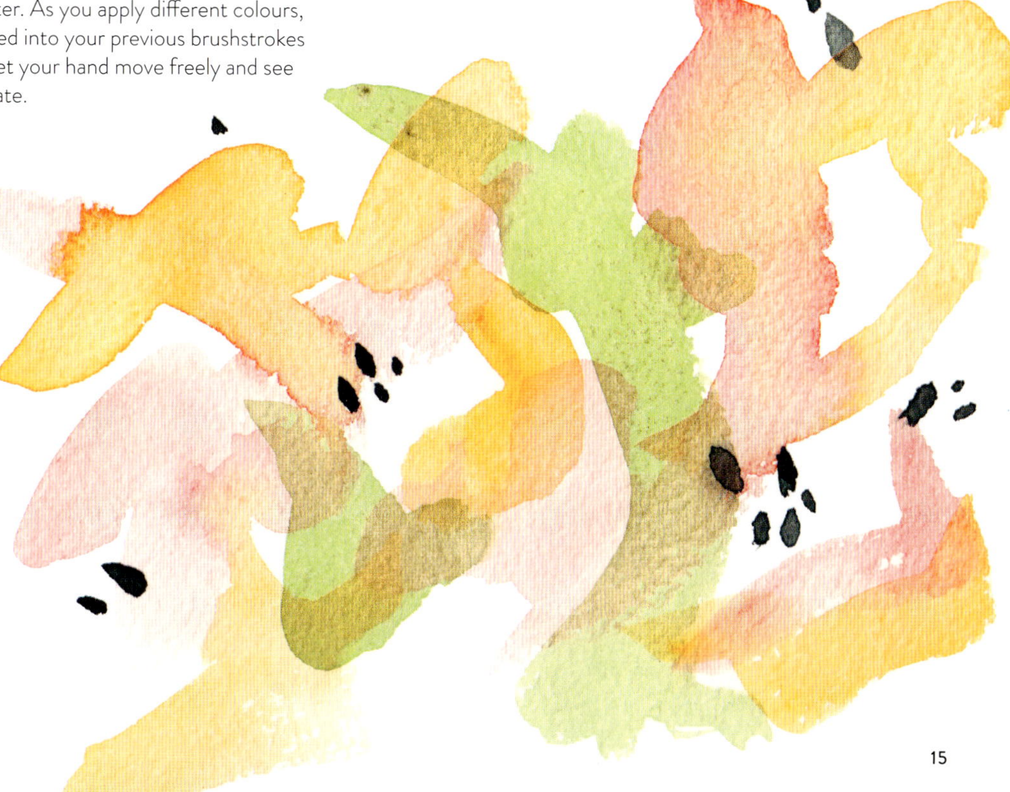

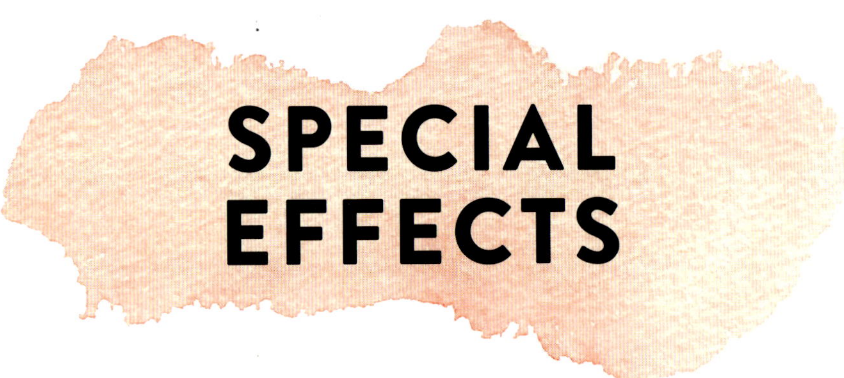

SPECIAL EFFECTS

Four paint effects with multiple applications

Don't try to control the paint excessively. Instead, learn to take advantage of watercolour's fluidity and looseness on the page.

Wet-on-wet and wet-on-dry are the two methods that you will use most in your watercolour painting. You can use each method on its own as well as mixing the two together. These exercises will show some of the effects that can be created by experimenting with water and its application.

17   PAINT SPLATTER

Paint splatter is a fun finishing touch to a painting (see pages 25 and 38). You can change the size of the splatters by using different size brushes and more or less water. The closer the brush is to the paper, the more dense your splatter will be; the further away the brush, the more diffuse the result. This technique is worked wet-on-dry.

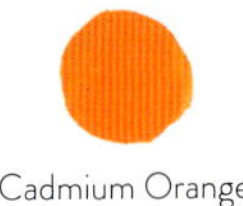

Cadmium Yellow and
Pyrrol Crimson

Cadmium Orange

1. Wet your brush and create a puddle of your chosen paint colour on your palette.

2. Load your brush with colour and hold it horizontally over the paper. Have your hand at the very end of the brush.

3. Using your free hand, tap the paintbrush several times with a pencil. Each tap will create a new splatter of paint.

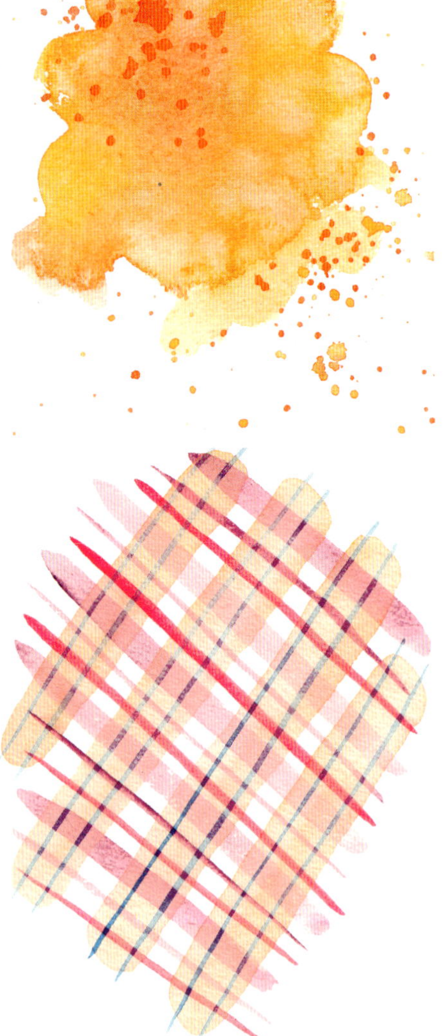

18   OVERLAPPING COLOUR

Create a swatch of tartan to see how several colours work together. This wet-on-dry technique allows you to see the new colours created when paints overlap. Choose a limited selection of colours to create your tartan check – the three primaries, for example.

Ultramarine Blue

Cadmium Yellow and
Pyrrol Crimson

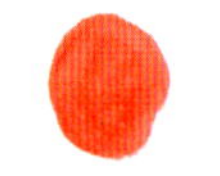

Pyrrol Crimson

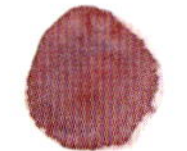

Ultramarine Blue and
Pyrrol Crimson

1. Use a large brush to create thick horizontal lines of your first colour, with spaces between them. Leave the paint to dry.

2. Add horizontal lines of your second colour between those of the first colour. Experiment with different line thicknesses, if you like.

3. Once all the horizontal lines are completely dry, paint vertical lines of your third colour over the top. Again, play around with the spacing.

19   WORKING WITH SALT

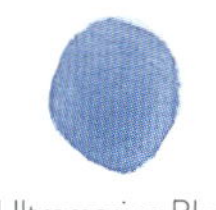

Cobalt Teal

Ultramarine Blue

Interesting effects result from sprinkling salt over wet watercolours. It's a technique that you can use to create a sponge-like texture to an area of your painting – to achieve a moss-like finish for vegetation or the foam on turbulent waters.

1.   Create a wash of colour on your paper using a large wet brush.
2.   While the paint is still very wet, sprinkle regular table salt over the top.
3.   Once dry, brush the salt from the paper to find some beautifully abstract results.

20   MARBLING

Ultramarine Blue

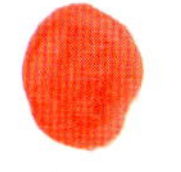

Cadmium Yellow and
Pyrrol Crimson

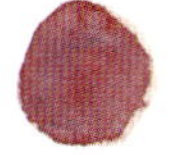

Pyrrol Crimson

Ultramarine Blue and
Pyrrol Crimson

This is a wet-on-wet technique that can be used for more controlled bleeding and blending of colours. Here it is used to create a series of distant planets.

1.   Using a pencil, lightly sketch several circles on your paper.
2.   Wet your brush and fill one circle with a wash of water.
3.   While the paper is still wet, dip a wet brush into your chosen colour and lightly dab the paint onto the circle of water. The paint will start to spread.
4.   Continue to dab paint onto the water, leaving space between each brush mark and switching colours if you wish to create a more distinct marbled effect.

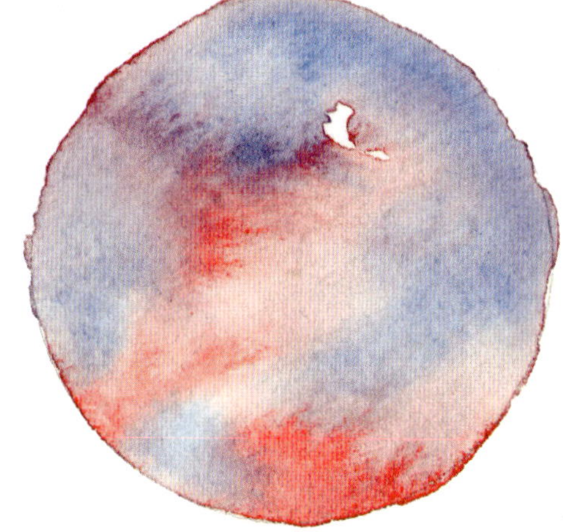

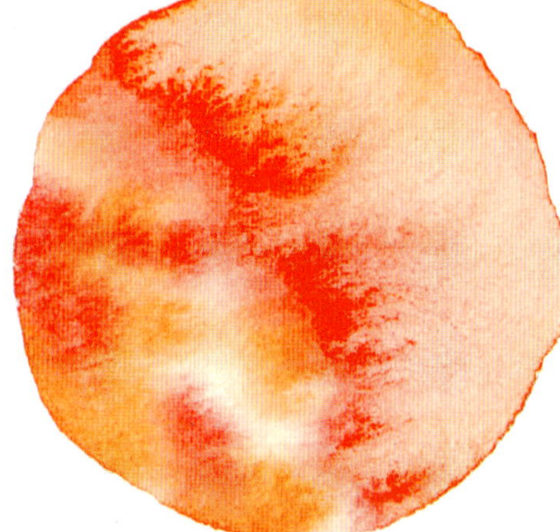

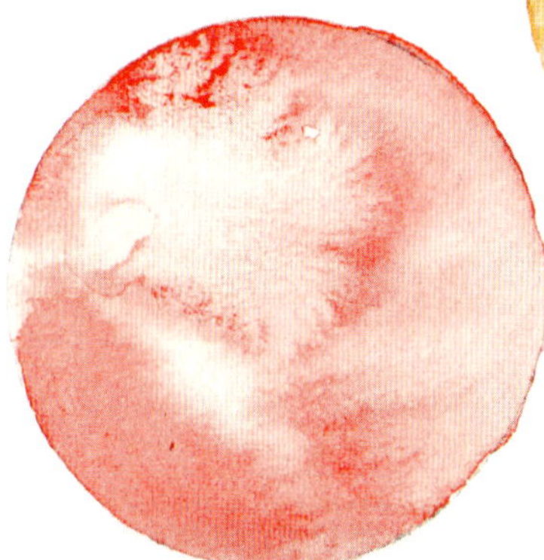

LETTING THE PAINT RUN

Three ways to play with water

Experimenting with fluidity is one of the most pleasing aspects of watercolour painting, and one step on from letting colours bleed (see pages 14–15) is to let the paint run in a certain direction. Although you cannot completely control what happens, this allows you to explore a little more creatively with the technique.

Here are three options for you to explore.

21 SCREW IT UP

Watercolour paint will always pool into any creases in your paper. Experiment with this tendency by scrunching up a piece of paper and then flattening it out once again. Then paint a large wash of very wet paint across the surface of the paper and leave it to dry while watching the paint settle.

22 ABSTRACT RUNS

Cadmium Yellow and Pyrrol Crimson

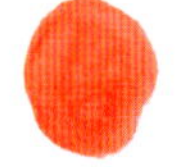

Pyrrol Crimson

Ultramarine Blue and Pyrrol Crimson

1. Use a very wet, flat paintbrush to paint a strip of colour across the paper.

2. While still wet add a second band of a different colour just beneath the first, and a third beneath that.

3. While all of the layers are still wet, stand the paper up vertically to allow drips to form. You can encourage this by lightly tapping the bottom edge of the paper against your worktop.

4. Experiment with vertical changes in colour. You could even create a city landscape or silhouette and add splatters of paint using the technique on page 16.

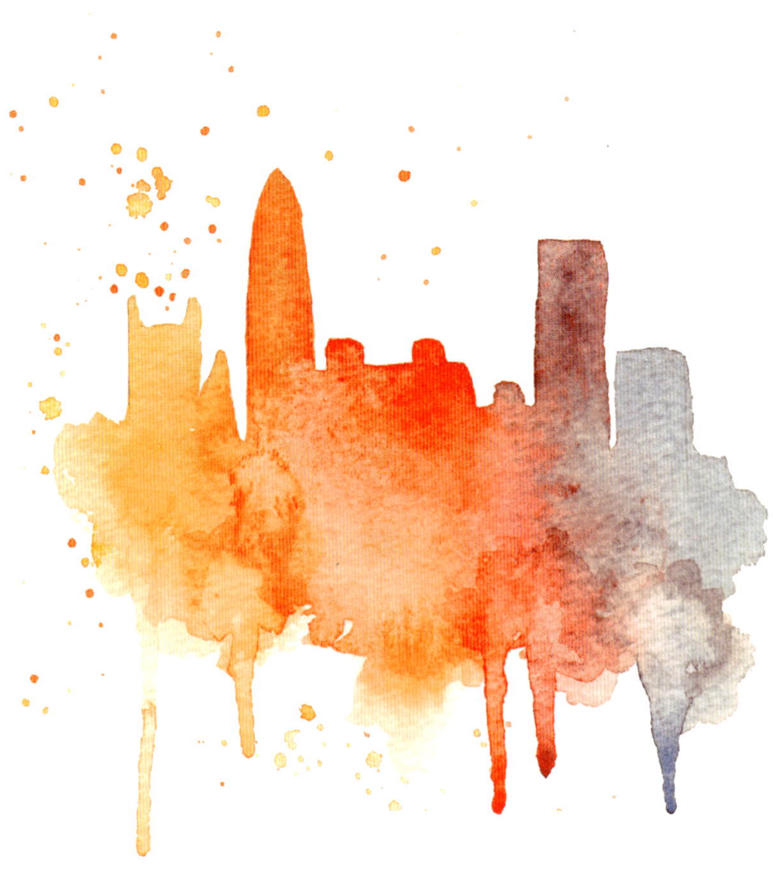

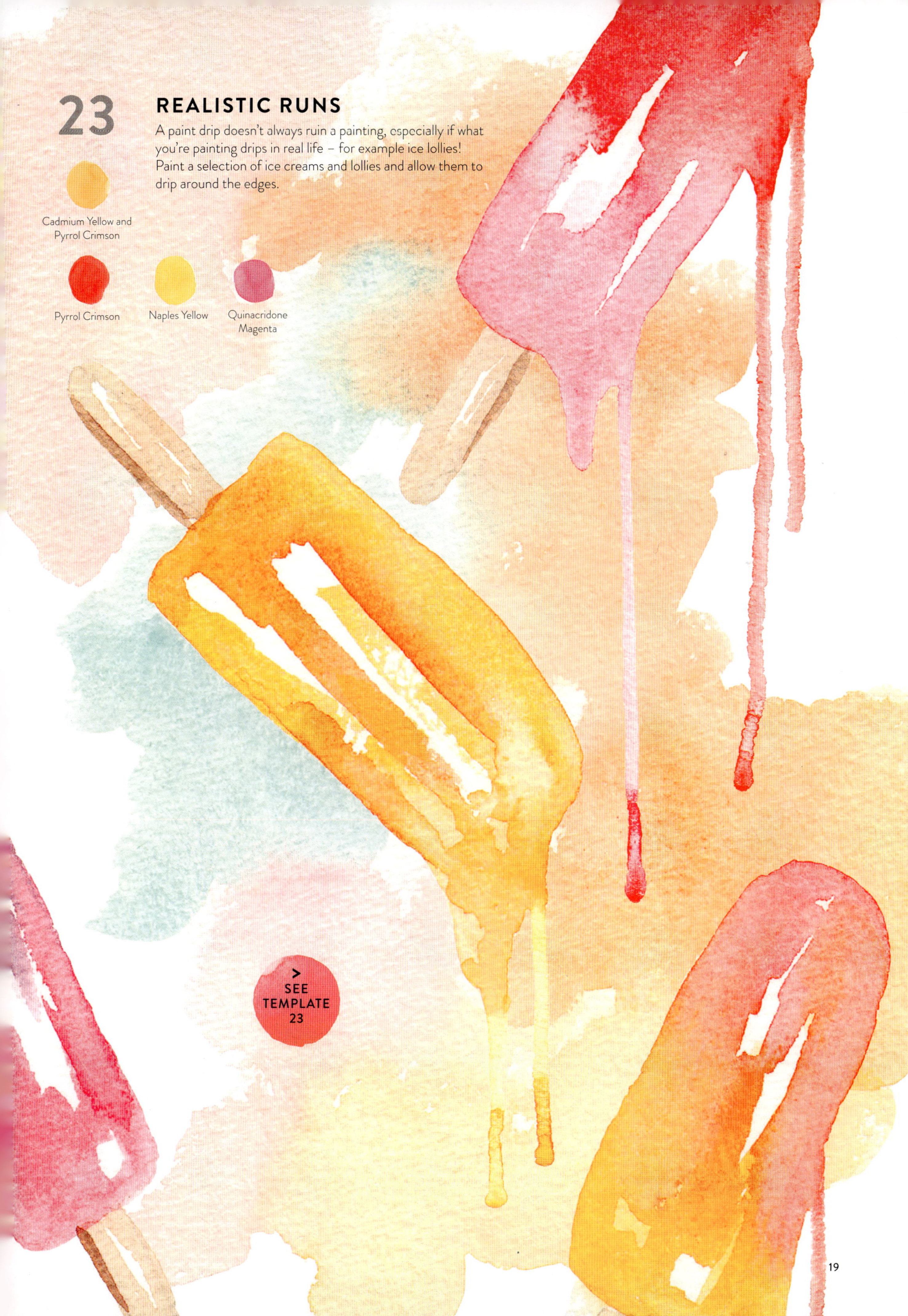

23 REALISTIC RUNS

A paint drip doesn't always ruin a painting, especially if what you're painting drips in real life – for example ice lollies! Paint a selection of ice creams and lollies and allow them to drip around the edges.

Cadmium Yellow and Pyrrol Crimson

Pyrrol Crimson

Naples Yellow

Quinacridone Magenta

BUILDING COLOUR

Three ways to build depth of colour

The technical term for the layering that forms the basis of all watercolour painting is 'glazing.' Each layer of paint is a 'glaze' and can be applied wet-on-wet or wet-on-dry.

The key to success is to be patient when allowing one layer to dry before painting the next and not to rush into subsequent layers. The various methods allow you to build colour subtly, without losing fine details.

24 SOFT GLAZING

Working wet-on-wet allows you to render softer, subtler finishes, such as those seen in the icing on doughnuts.

1. Paint the base layer – in this case, the main colour of the icing.

2. While the paint is wet, apply more paint of the same colour where the shadows fall – typically on the edge furthest from the light and to one side of the doughnut hole.

3. Use a dry brush to tease the edges of this second layer of paint, blending any hard edges where the two layers overlap.

4. Leave the icing section to dry completely before adding any sprinkle details. This is important to prevent the decoration colours from bleeding into the icing.

Serpentine Genuine

Alizarin Crimson

Ultramarine Blue

Cadmium Yellow

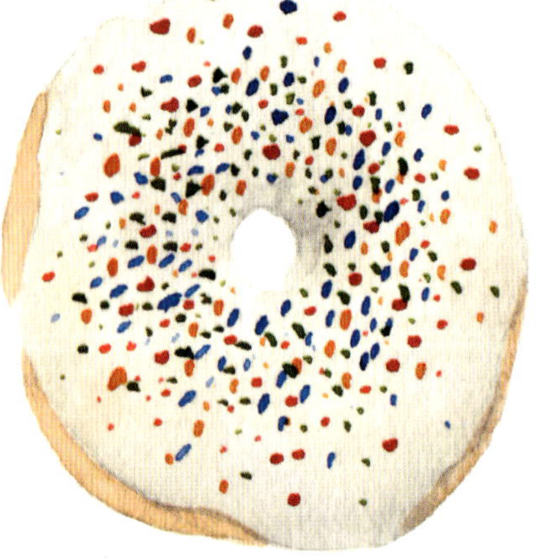

25

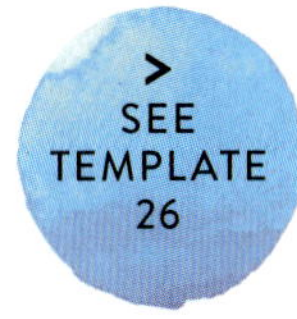

Deep Ochre

Cadmium Yellow

Cadmium Orange

Sap Green

LAYERING FOR BOLD COLOUR

For bold outlines and colours, as in these minibeasts, opt for a wet-on-dry method when glazing, leaving each layer to dry fully before painting the next.

1. Always start with the lightest shades of colour – that is, with more water on your brush. Use these to paint the full outlines of your subjects.

2. Once that is dry you can begin to add another layer of detail – for instance, the veins in a butterfly's wings.

3. Only when all layers are completely dry should you add the boldest details, such as legs, wing patterns and antennae.

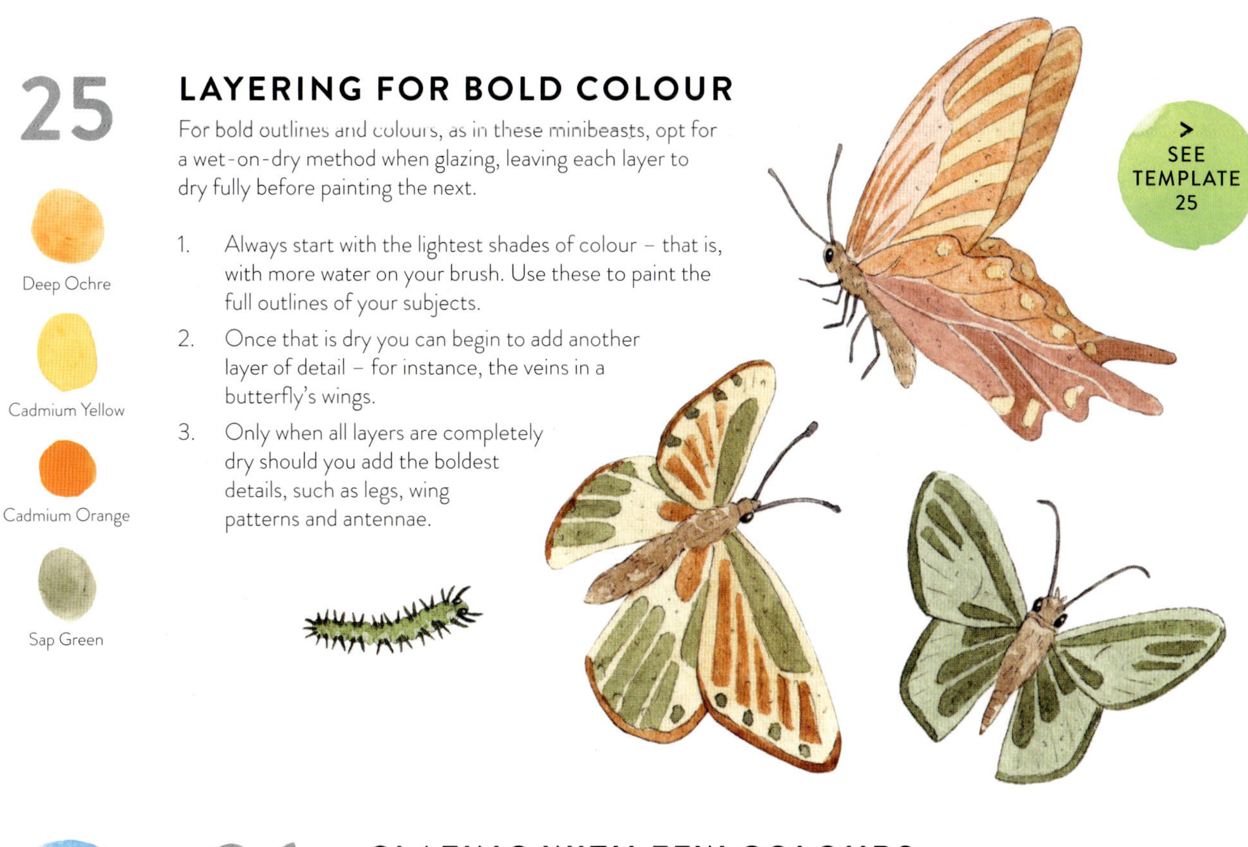

26

Yellow Ochre

Cadmium Yellow and
Pyrrol Crimson

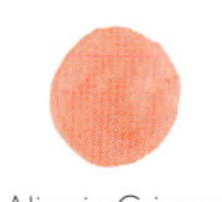

Alizarin Crimson

GLAZING WITH FEW COLOURS

Rather than applying thick brushstrokes of paint, build on the drawing and layering techniques you learned on pages 10, 12 and 13 to build colour gradually. This fish piece uses a limited palette to demonstrate the effects more clearly.

1. Begin with the lightest colour, in this case a pale yellow or orange. This is the base colour. Use it to paint the outlines of the fish and lay a first wash.

2. Once dry, paint over some areas of each fish using a slightly darker yellow or orange. Leave the base colour visible here and there as highlights.

3. Wait for each layer to dry before starting the next, gradually working up to the darkest details.

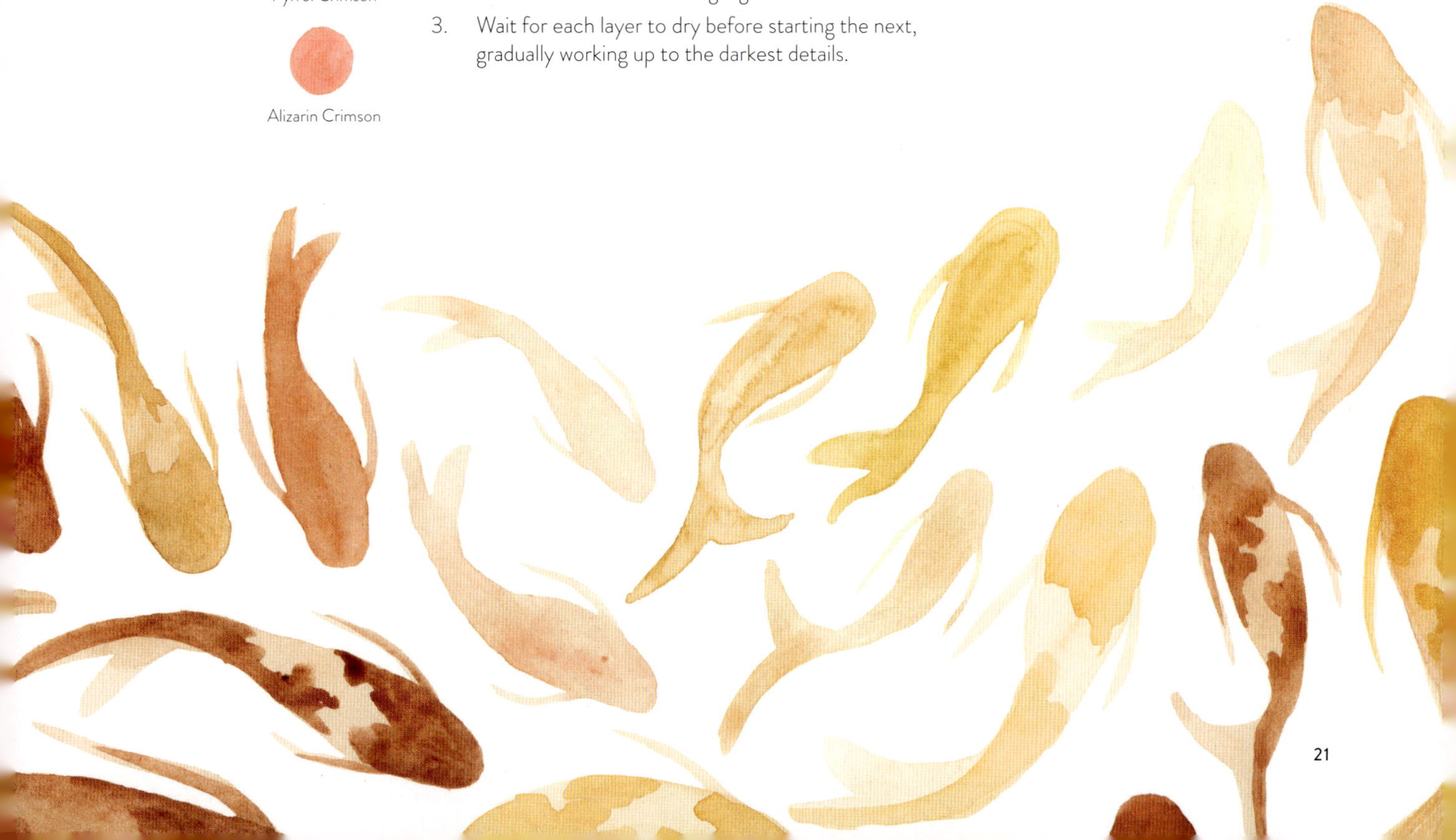

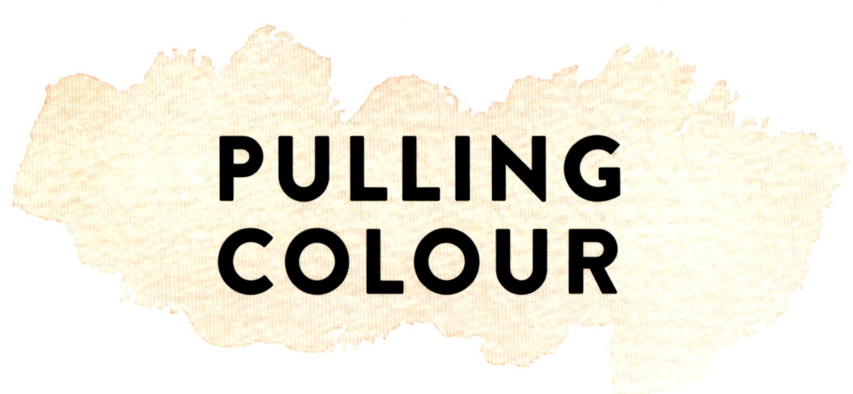
PULLING COLOUR

Three uses for the pulling technique

Pulling colour involves manipulating paint while it is still wet. It's a technique with several applications, one of which is to soften harsh edges that form when using the wet-on-dry method of glazing.

Working the paint with a wet brush enables you to soften the brushstrokes to achieve a smooth gradient finish. In this way, pulling can be used to form shadows and to emphasize the three-dimensionality of an object.

27

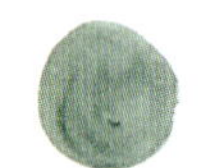

Perylene Green

Green Gold

Sap Green

FORMING SHADOWS

1. Plants, leaves and stems make good subjects for pulling colour in order to create shadows. Paint a leaf cluster or sprig using a light green.

2. Once the base layer is dry, apply a dark shade of green where shadows fall – where a leaf meets the stem, for example.

3. Using a clean, wet brush pull the dark paint away from the plant stem and toward the tip of a leaf.

4. When the painting is dry, you will have created a smooth gradient from dark to light.

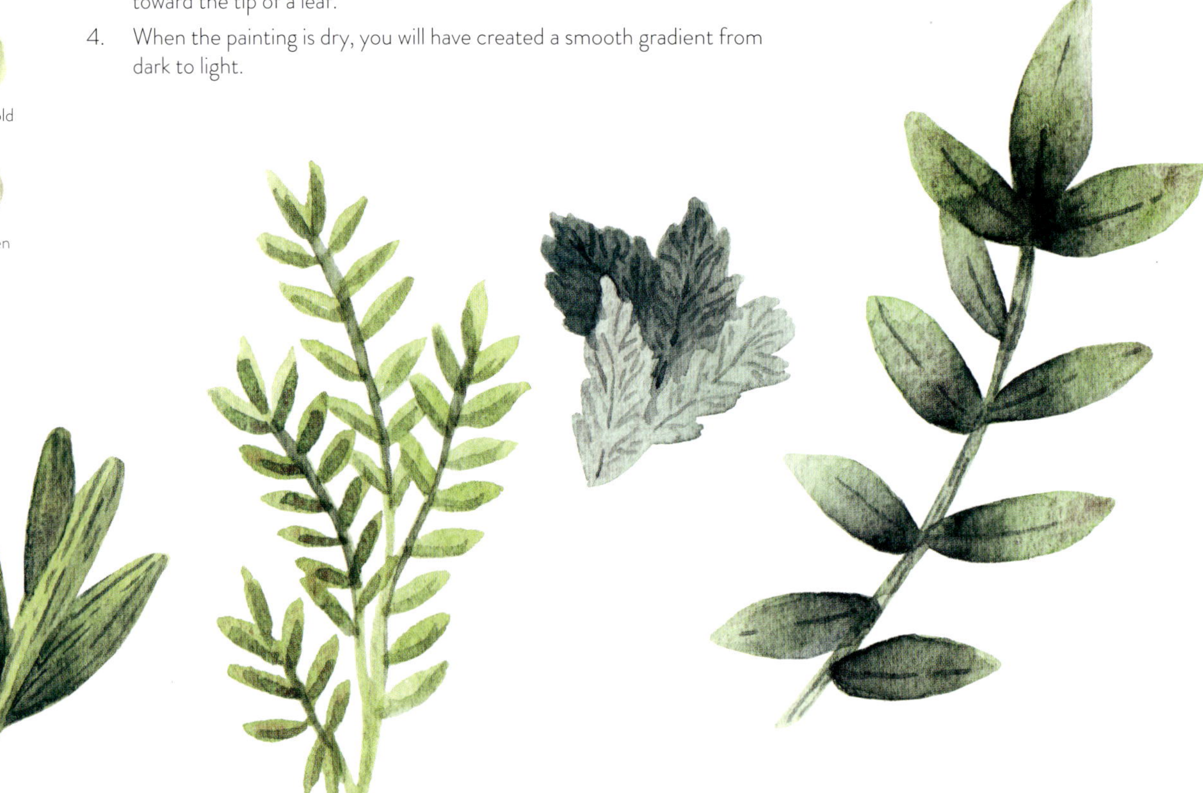

28 THREE-DIMENSIONALITY

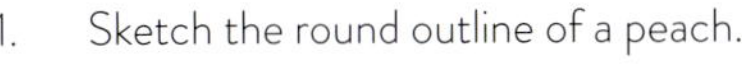

You can pull one colour over a layer of a different colour to create soft colour changes. In the case of this peach, the technique helps to give the fruit depth and form.

1. Sketch the round outline of a peach.
2. Create a wash of orange to fill the peach shape and leave it to dry.
3. In places, paint a dark pink stroke around the outside edge of the peach.
4. Use a clean, wet brush to pull the pink paint towards the center of the peach, leaving some of the orange layer visible beneath.

Alizarin Crimson

Naples Yellow

Green Gold

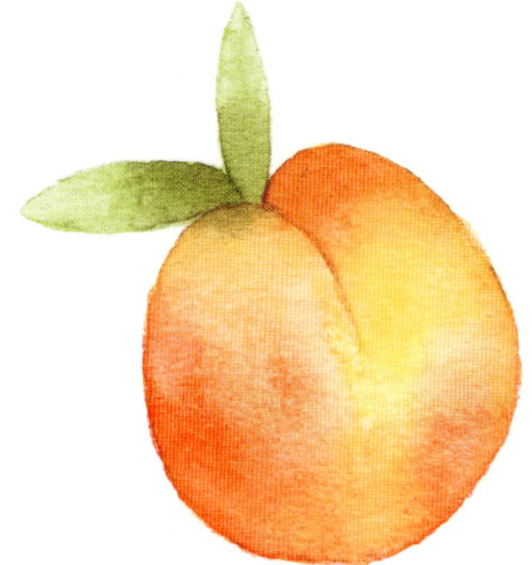

29 CREATING SHAPE AND TEXTURE

You can use the pulling technique to emphasize changes in shape and texture. Pumpkins make great subjects for this, with their undulating shapes.

1. Sketch the outline of a pumpkin, and very finely sketch the individual segments.
2. Create a wash of a pale orange or yellow to fill the pumpkin and leave it to dry.
3. Using darker colours, and working on each segment in turn, apply paint at the base of each segment.
4. Immediately use a clean, wet brush to pull the paint part way up the segment, to give it greater definition.

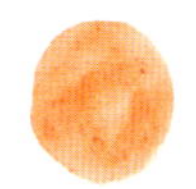

Pompeii Red

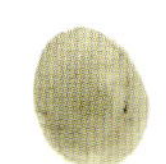

Sap Green

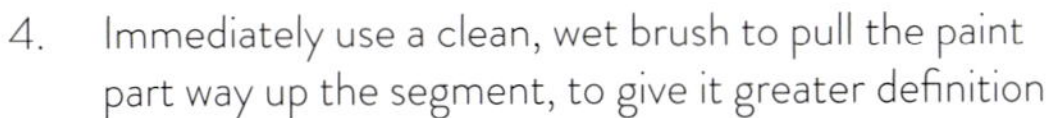

Cadmium Yellow

Cadmium Orange

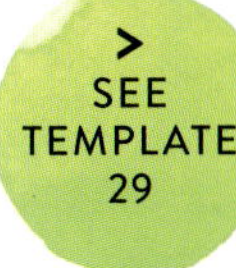

> SEE TEMPLATE 29

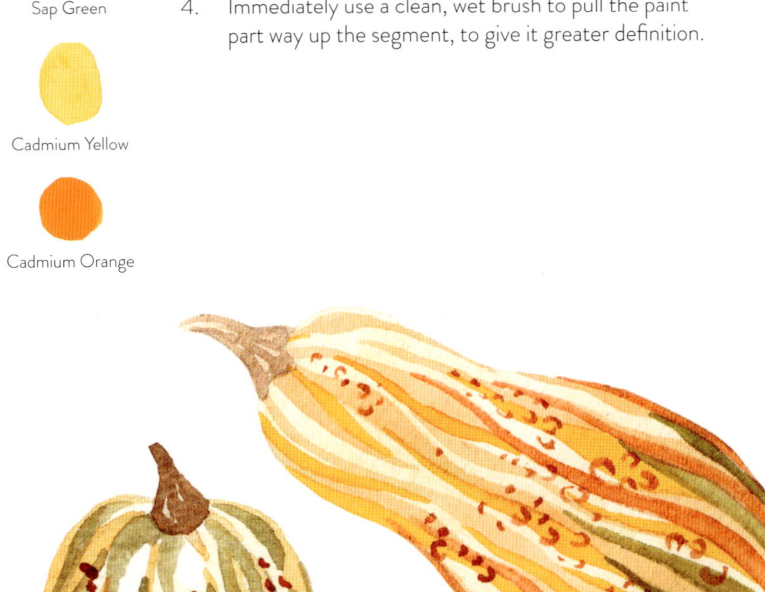

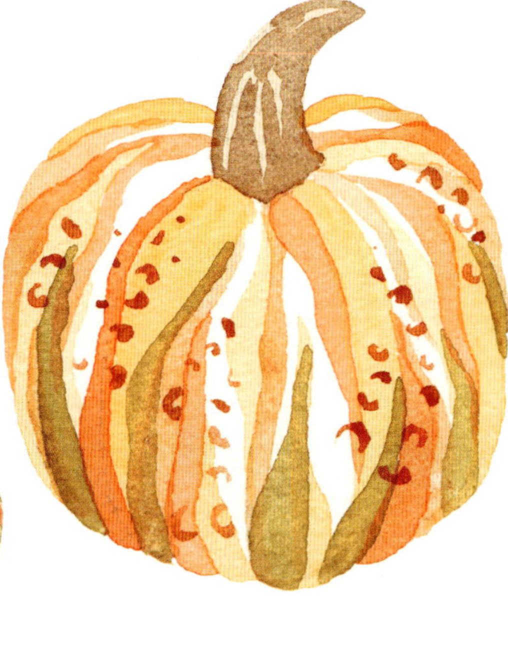

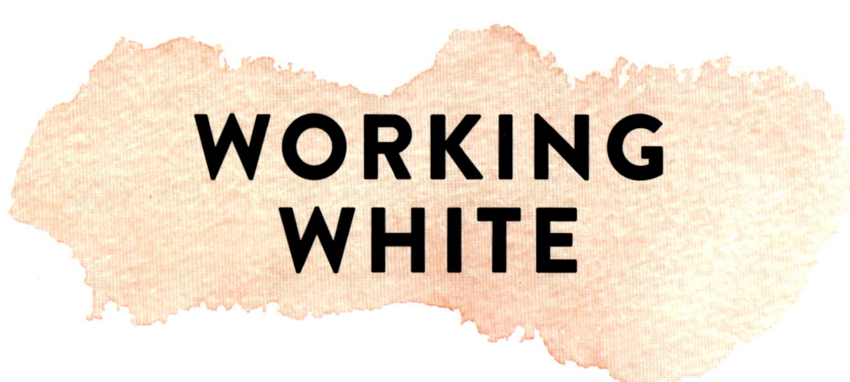

Four ways to manipulate the white of your paper

These exercises build on the jellyfish project on page 13, and demonstrate other ways in which to use the white of the paper as a feature of your painting.

The four techniques shown here can be applied in many different ways, depending on your subject matter. For all of them, it is crucial that you decide which areas of the paper need to stay white right from the start.

30 NEGATIVE PAINTING

This is a novel technique that mirrors the effect of a photographic negative – the subject remains white, while the background takes on colour. Apply this technique using something that has an intricate outline, such as a feather.

1. Sketch the outline of the feather.
2. Keeping the interior of the sketch untouched, fill the rest of the paper in any way you choose to create an abstract background.
3. You'll have created a negative painting with the perfect silhouette of a feather.

31 MASKING TAPE

Masking tape is often used in watercolour, to form a neat edge around a painting. You can also use it to create the painting in the first place, as here.

1. Lay strips of masking tape across your paper to create a criss-cross geometric pattern. Apply reasonably light pressure, as you'll be removing the tape later.
2. Paint the shapes that fall between the strips of tape. Use block colours, patterns or different watercolour effects.
3. Allow the painting to dry completely before removing the masking tape.

Ultramarine Blue

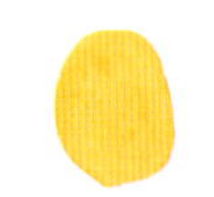
Cadmium Yellow

Cadmium Yellow and Pyrrol Crimson

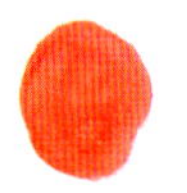
Pyrrol Crimson

Ultramarine Blue and Pyrrol Crimson

Cobalt Teal

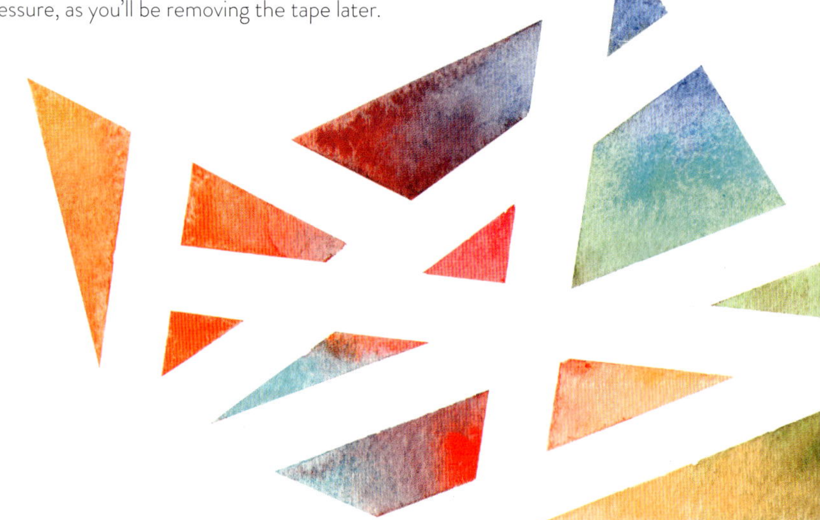

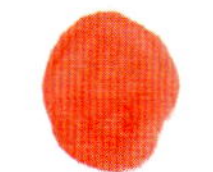

32

MASKING FLUID

Masking fluid is perfect for creating intricate white highlights in a painting.

1. Apply fluid to the places that you want to keep white and leave it to dry completely.

2. Continue with your painting. Don't worry if you paint over the masking fluid, it will resist the paint.

3. Once the paint is dry, lightly rub the hardened fluid with your finger or a rubber to make it peel away from the paper leaving the perfect white highlights intact.

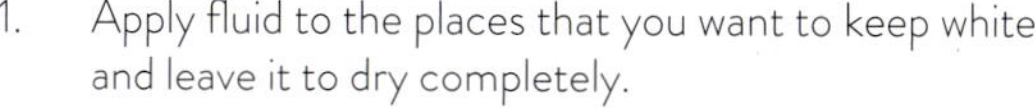

Pyrrol Crimson

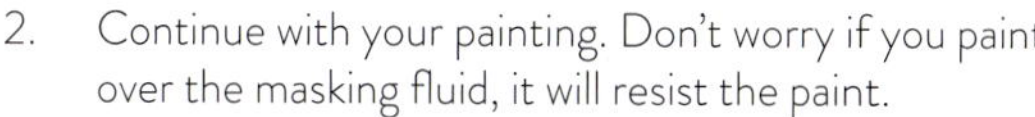

Ultramarine Blue and
Pyrrol Crimson

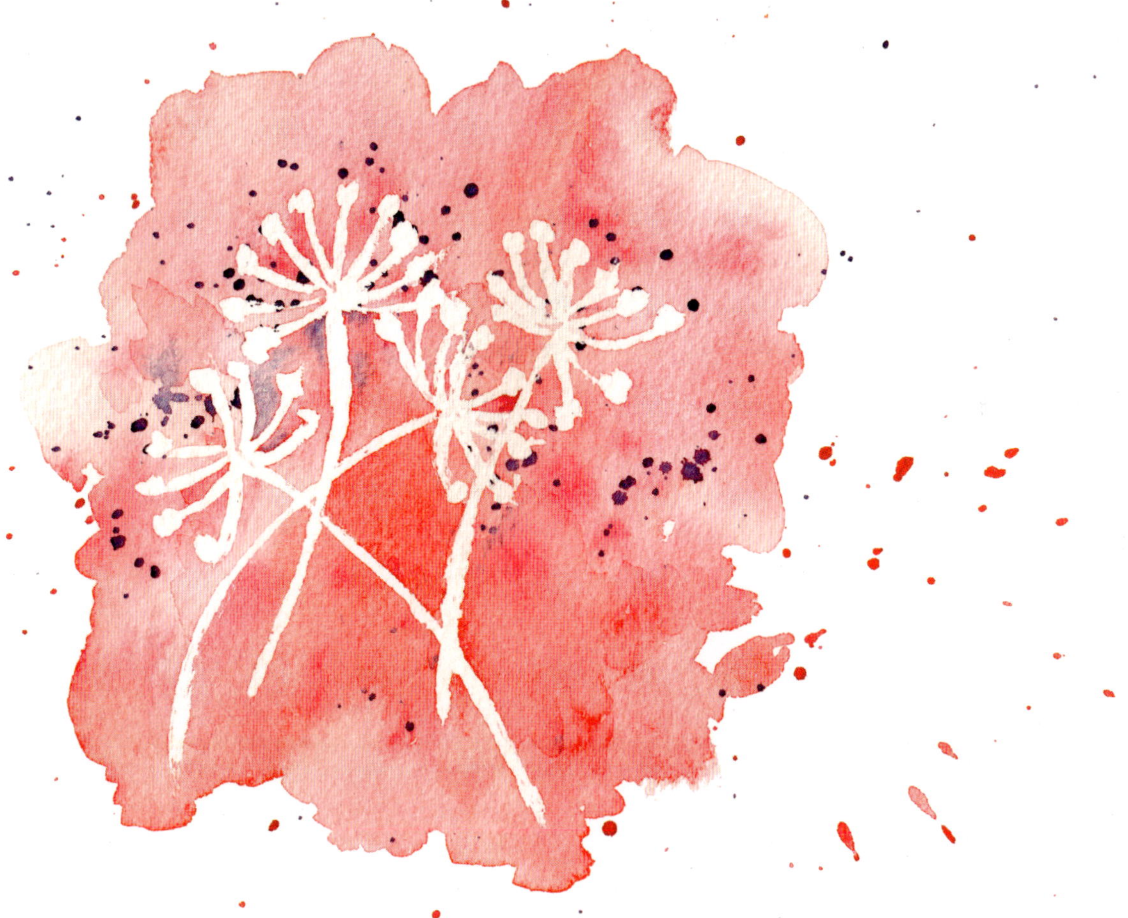

33

LIGHT AS REFLECTIONS

You can create highlights that gradually blend into shadow using the pulling technique described on page 22. Crystals make a great study for this, as their many faceted surfaces reflect light in all directions.

1. Lightly sketch your crystal, complete with each of its geometric protruding shapes.

2. Decide on the areas that will show as reflections and therefore need to stay white.

3. As you build the layers of colour, experiment with the pulling technique to remove any harsh edges, to make the highlights really pop.

Ultramarine Blue

Cobalt Teal

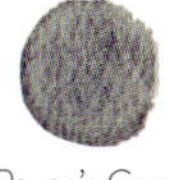

Payne's Grey

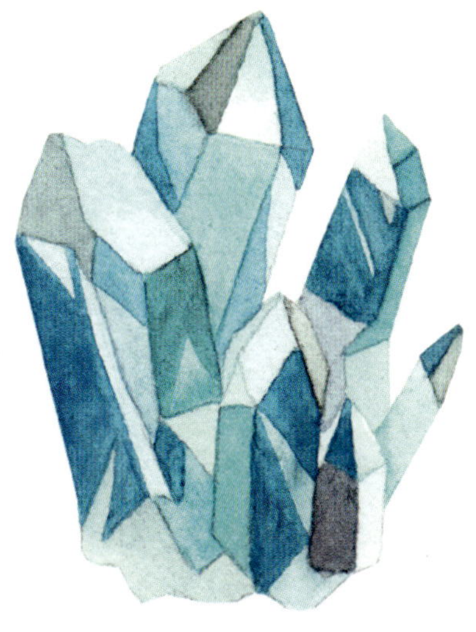

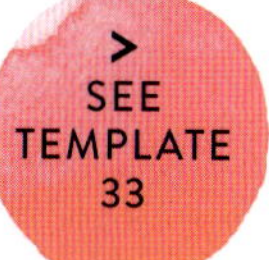

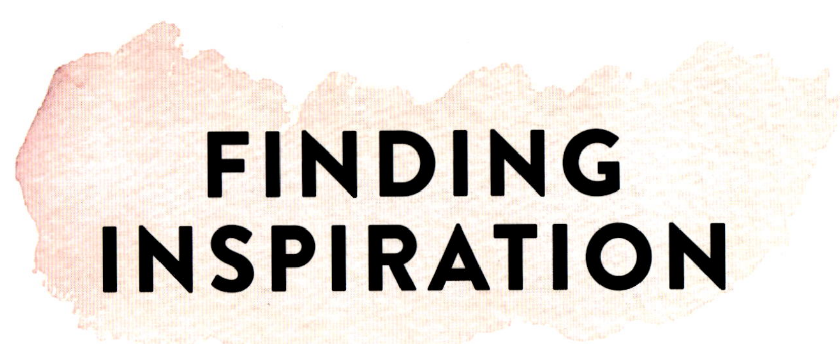

FINDING INSPIRATION

Three on-the-spot ways to find inspiration

You may have plenty of ideas for the paintings you want to create, but there will inevitably be times when you struggle over your subject matter. Here are some creative ways around the problem.

Challenge your mind to think outside the box, for example, by turning to ink-blot painting or by simply painting anything that is close to hand.

34

Quinacrido Magenta

Cadmium Yellow

Cobalt Teal

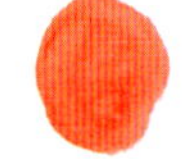

Pyrrol Crimson

Sap Green

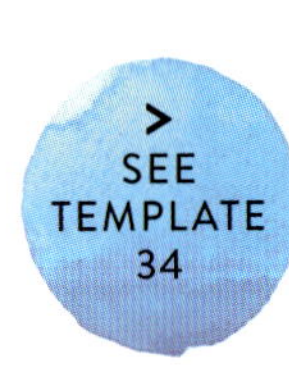

HIRAMEKI

Hirameki is Japanese for 'flash of inspiration.' It's a form of ink-blot painting that encourages you to change the way you look at things, making it a great antidote to creative block.

1. Paint a number of random blobs, smears, splodges and splashes on your paper, in a range of different colours. Leave them to dry.

2. Using a pen, consider each shape and simply draw what you see. Reimagine that splat as a new shape – a smiling man, a whale, a palm tree or a fish, for example.

3. Add details with your pen to really bring the shape to life.

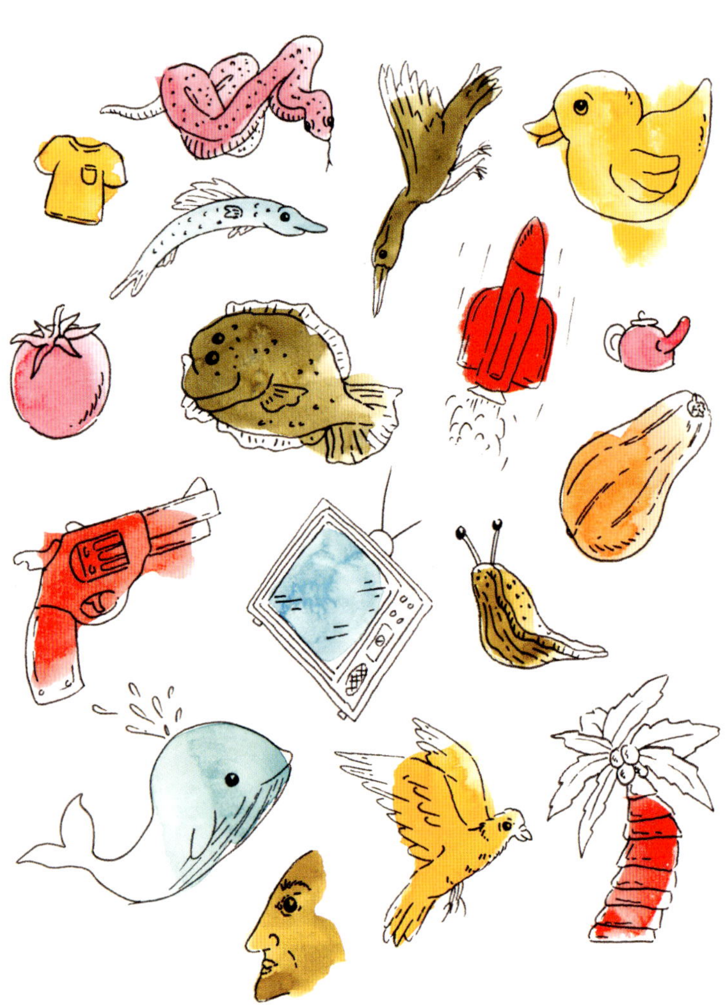

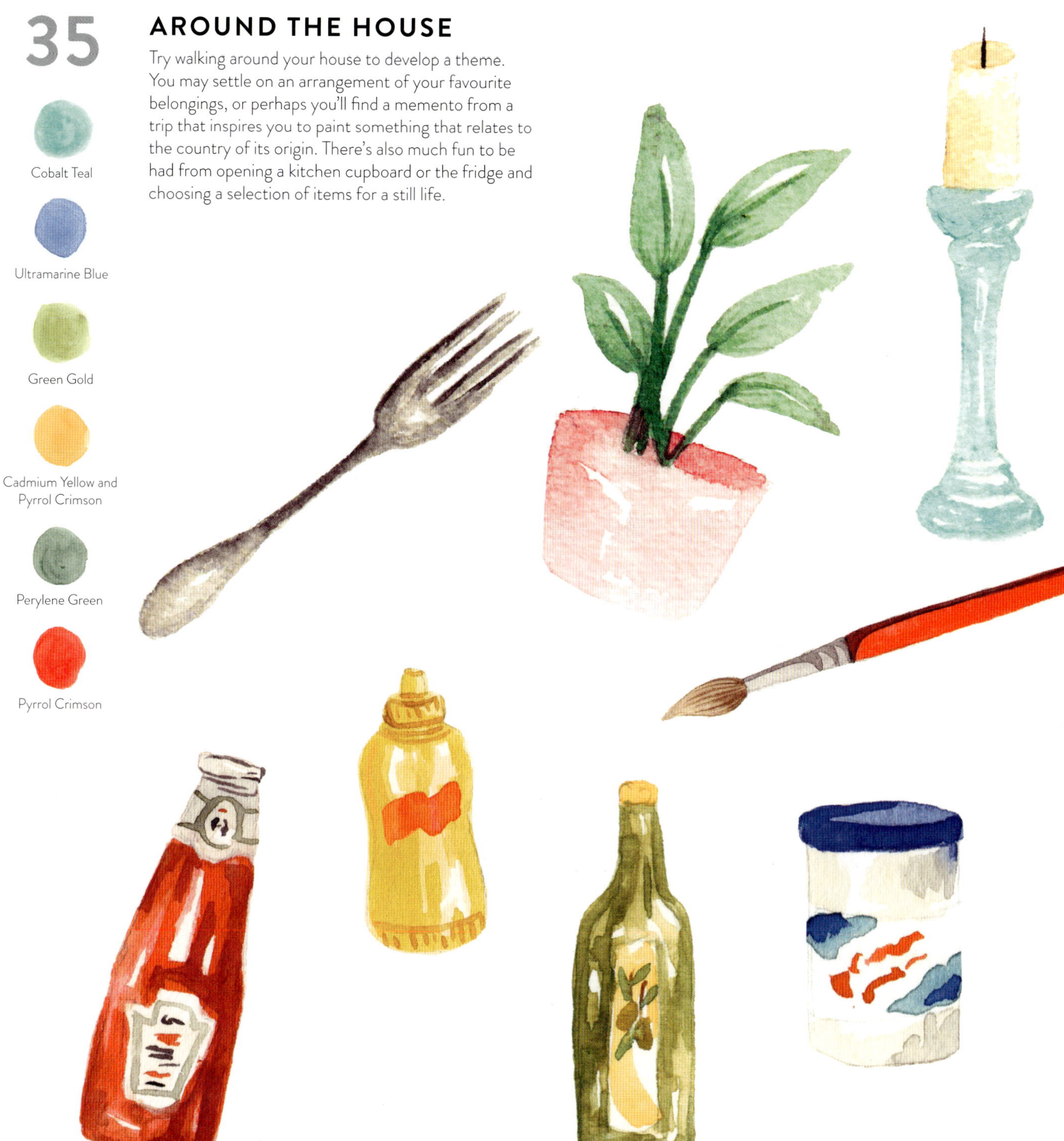

35   AROUND THE HOUSE

Try walking around your house to develop a theme. You may settle on an arrangement of your favourite belongings, or perhaps you'll find a memento from a trip that inspires you to paint something that relates to the country of its origin. There's also much fun to be had from opening a kitchen cupboard or the fridge and choosing a selection of items for a still life.

36   STEP OUTSIDE

Why not step into the garden or take a short walk in your neighbourhood? There's no end to the scenes that you could snap on your phone for reference. Or perhaps assemble a few pebbles or a posy of wildflowers that offer interesting shapes and colours.

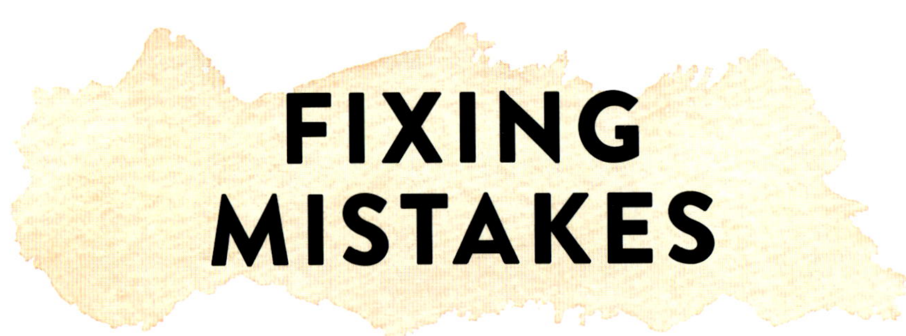

FIXING MISTAKES

Three creative ways to deal with mistakes

It's important to realize that most 'mistakes' in your paintings won't be seen by anyone else and really aren't a problem. But if there are some mistakes that have left you utterly fed up, here are some techniques that will help you get past them.

It's quite likely that after spending hours on a painting and then accidentally dropping your paint brush and creating an unwanted mark, you could become a little irritated. However, this kind of mistake is fairly inevitable. Although you can't get the paper back to a pure white, it's possible to lift the colour in order to erase a mistake. If the paint is already dry, use a clean, wet brush to paint over the area. Leave it to settle for a little while and then, before it dries, blot the area with a paper towel. The towel will absorb the water you added, along with pigment from the layer beneath.

37 LIFTING TO CREATE A HIGHLIGHT

Although you can't get your paper back to a pure white, it's possible to lift colour in order to add highlights that you failed to consider at the planning stage. Follow this raspberry demonstration to see how.

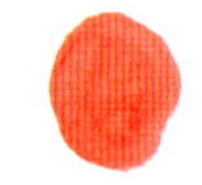

Pyrrol Crimson

Green Gold

1. Begin by layering washes to form the shape of a raspberry. Intentionally omit some of the highlights.

2. Once the paint is dry, use a clean, wet brush to dab the fruit where you would like to add a highlight, leaving a bead of water.

3. Allow the water to settle for a few minutes and then remove the water and some of the pigment by blotting with a paper towel.

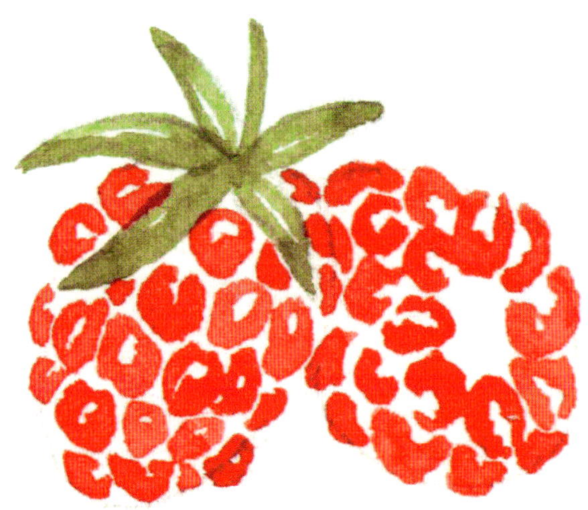

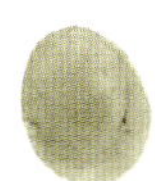

Sap Green

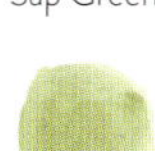

Green Gold

Perylene Green

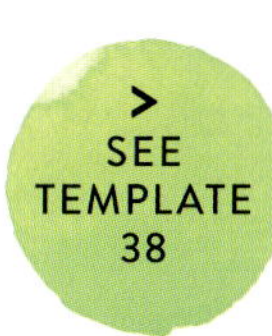

SPONGE WORK

You can use a normal household sponge to both lift and apply paint. To lift paint, wet the sponge and apply a little pressure as you dab the paper to remove colour. This works best if the paint is still slightly wet. Alternatively, if you have been left with a brushstroke or splatter that doesn't quite work, you can use a sponge to cover it up. Mix your paint with some water in a small dish and dip the sponge into it before dabbing the paper. This is particularly useful technique when working on texture. A wetter sponge works best for creating and correcting clouds and water effects, for example, whereas a drier sponge may create and correct a scaly effect, as here.

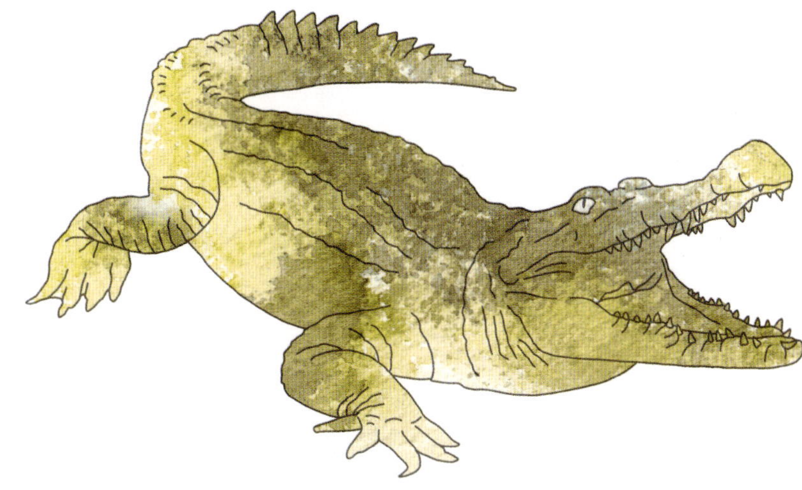

39

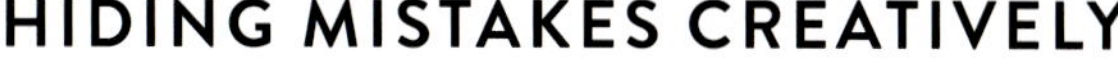

HIDING MISTAKES CREATIVELY

Perhaps, instead of jumping straight to covering a mistake, you could turn the mistake into something else. Think back to the Hirameki activity on page 26 and use the same technique to create something completely new.

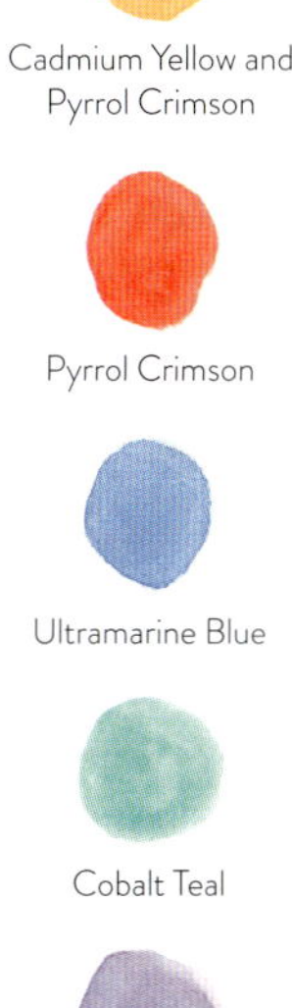

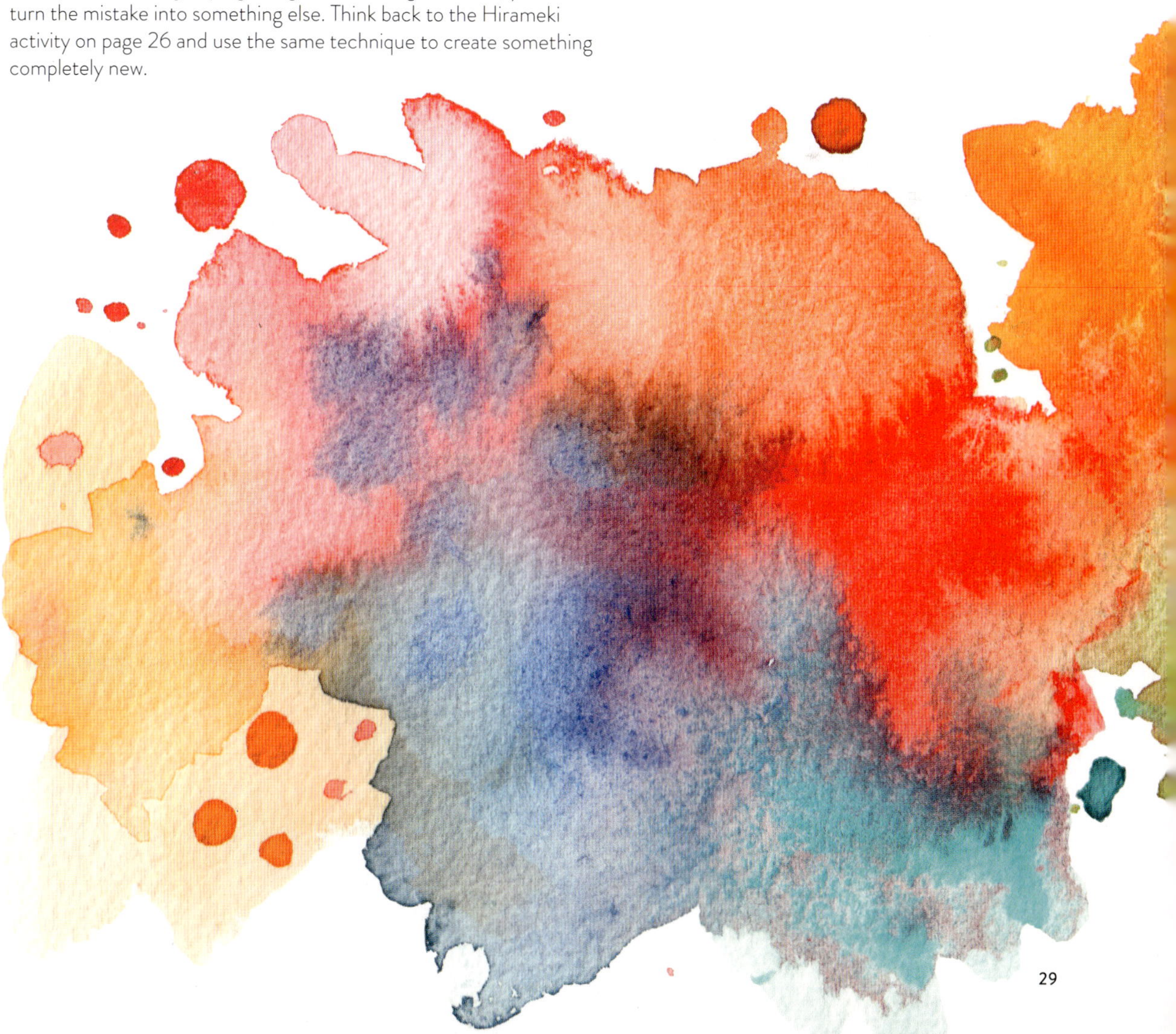

Cadmium Yellow and
Pyrrol Crimson

Pyrrol Crimson

Ultramarine Blue

Cobalt Teal

Ultramarine Blue and
Pyrrol Crimson

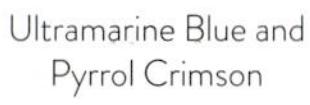

Green Gold

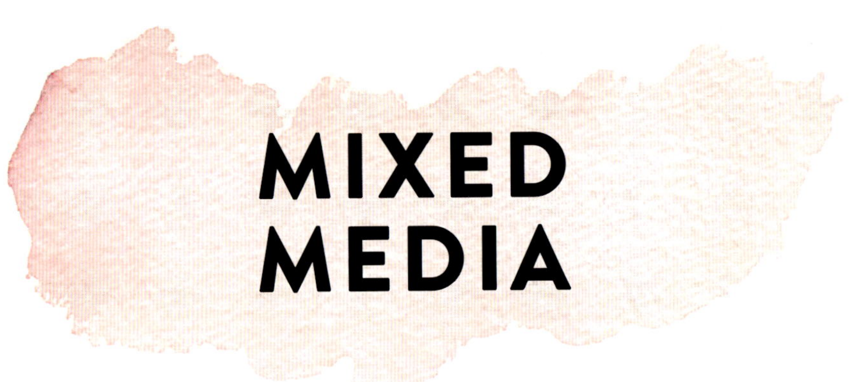

MIXED MEDIA

Three ways in which to use more than one medium

Watercolour is a versatile medium that works brilliantly when combined with other materials, particularly when it comes to achieving certain textural finishes or very fine details. The most successful pairings are graphite, colour pencils, gouache and pen. Generally each of these are applied after you have finished painting, although some fine liners work brilliantly when they are used before applying paint.

Try the following demonstrations to see which appeal most to you.

40 COLOUR PENCILS

Colour pencils are most effective when added after paint. Unlike watercolour pencils, they will not blend with the paint and are great for adding more depth and texture. After creating a wash, leave the paint to dry thoroughly. Rather than covering large areas, use the pencils to create small scribbles and crosshatchings.

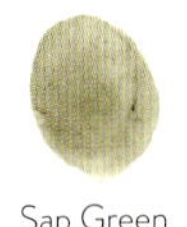

Sap Green

Green Gold

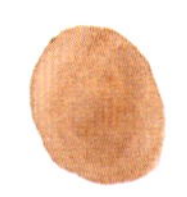

Yellow Ochre

Vandyke Brown

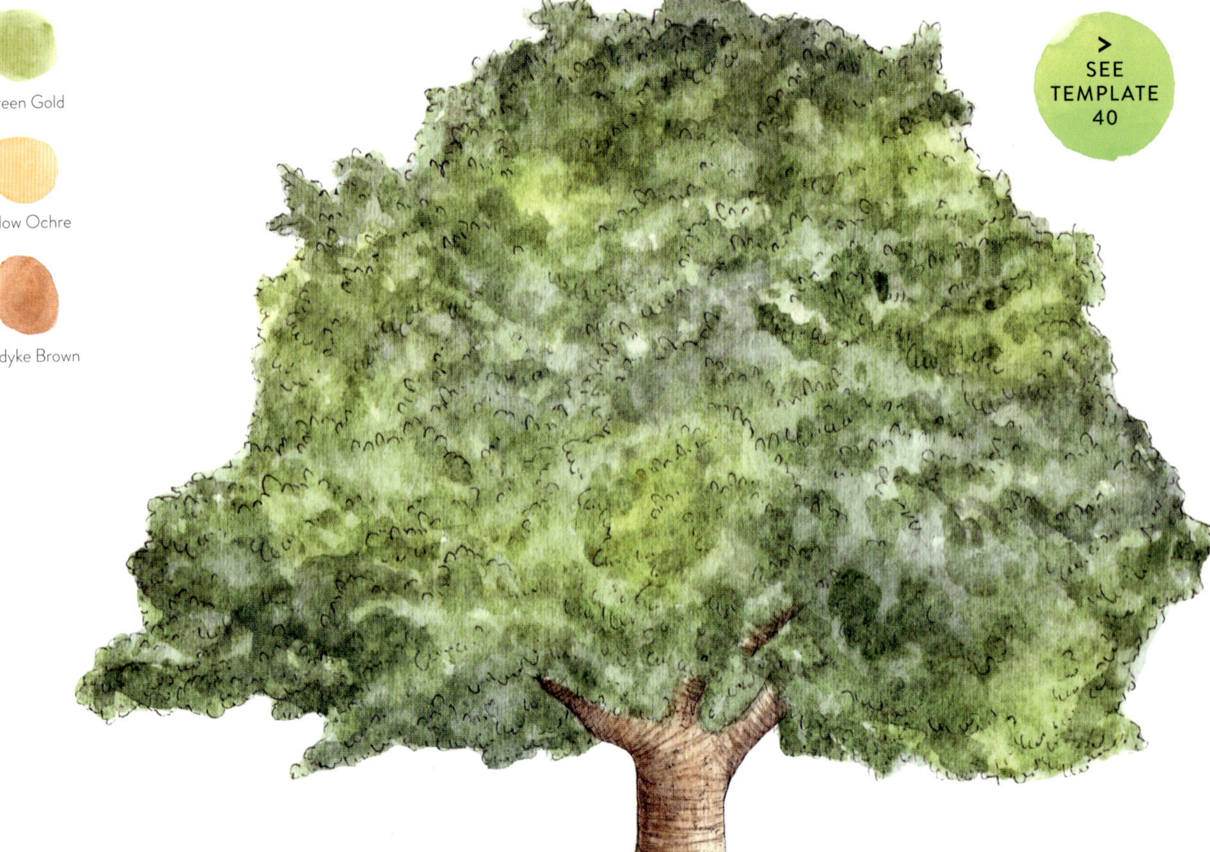

41 GOUACHE

Ultramarine Blue

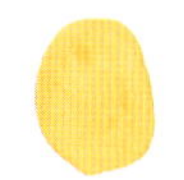

Cadmium Yellow

Cobalt Teal

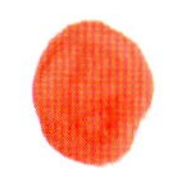

Pyrrol Crimson

Gouache is wonderful to paint with, particularly if you're looking to introduce a little opacity to a piece of work. It's made very similarly to watercolour but with a lot more pigment. It also contains chalk, which is what makes it flat and opaque. A very useful shade of gouache to own is white. It's perfect for adding any highlights you accidentally painted over and can add more punch than the paper white. It is best for your watercolours to be completely dry before adding gouache.

42 PEN

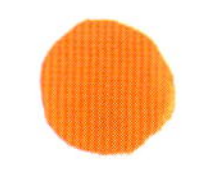

Cadmium Orange

Deep Ochre

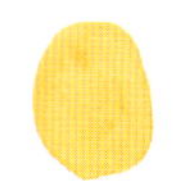

Cadmium Yellow

Naples Yellow

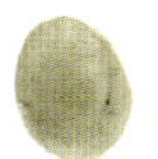

Sap Green

Green Gold

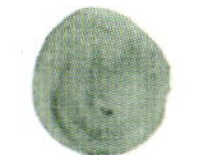

Perylene Green

Penwork can enhance details, add textures and contrasts and sharpen lines. Useful pen techniques include crosshatching, contour lines and stippling. These can be grouped together or spread apart. You should only add pen to watercolour once it is completely dry, although some fine liners are waterproof and can be used prior to painting (see pages 35 and 39).

1. Crosshatching simply involves intersecting parallel lines. Diagonal lines tend to create better shape.

2. Contour lines help define the edges of a subject.

3. Stippling involves adding dots of specks.

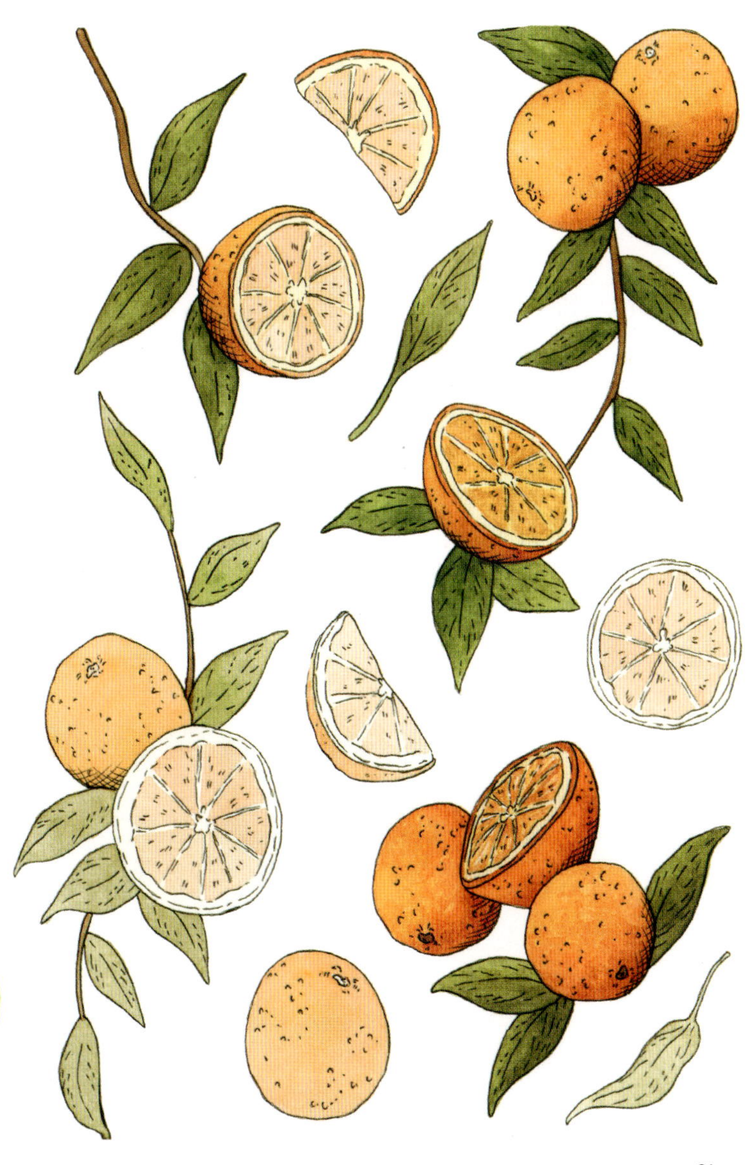

CHANNELLING YOUR THOUGHTS

Three steps to overcoming perfectionism or self doubt

It's very easy to become disheartened and give up on a painting because it doesn't match the image in your head. But becoming a better painter is learning to embrace the unexpected and to go with the flow. The beauty of watercolour is that it suits a loose and organic approach.

The following exercises will help you learn to let go of your preconceptions and redirect your energies towards viewing your work more positively.

43   REPEAT AND DIVERGE

Try letting go of the need for uniformity by painting the same object over and over again.

Ultramarine Blue

Cobalt Teal

1. Paint a perfect spiral, putting your all into making it symmetrical and balanced.

2. Repeat, but work a little faster and with less emphasis on perfection.

3. Continue to paint spirals, getting faster and faster as you go. By the time you have painted a dozen you'll see the beautiful variety that a looser approach can create.

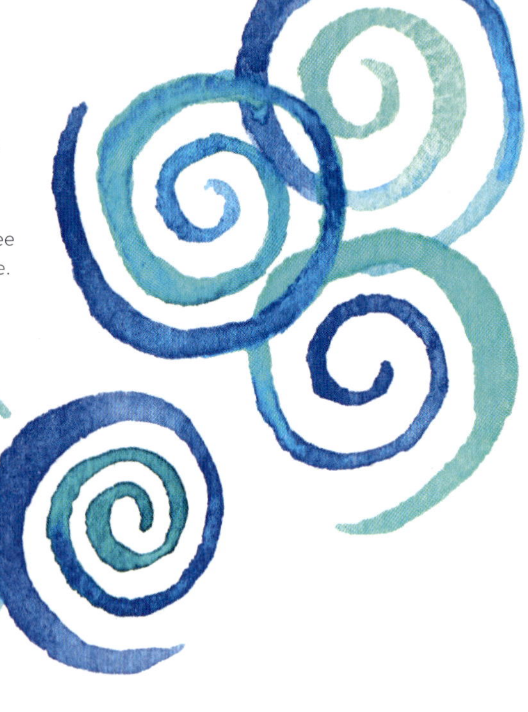

44   IT'S NEVER FINISHED

Overworking a painting is a common mistake and it's so hard to stop yourself from adding to it, particularly if you're not very happy with what you've painted. When you have moments like this, put your painting aside and grab a clean sheet of paper. Take your mind off the painting so that you can come back to it with fresh eyes. With your fresh piece, try some brush exercises to calm yourself. Create simple spirals with the brush, warming up your wrist and improving the steadiness of your strokes.

IDEAS OVERLOAD

Here, the problem doesn't lie in finding an idea, but having so many ideas that you don't know where to start. It can be helpful to write down all of your ideas in a notebook, or to try illustrating them as sketches to see which might work best. Alternatively, paint just one item to represent each of the themes you'd like to paint.

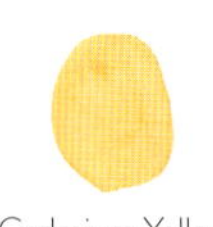

Cadmium Yellow

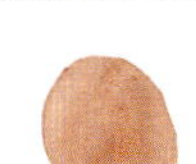

Vandyke Brown

Deep Ochre

Yellow Ochre

Indian Red

Ultramarine Blue

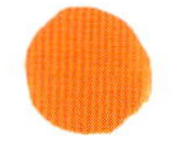

Cadmium Orange

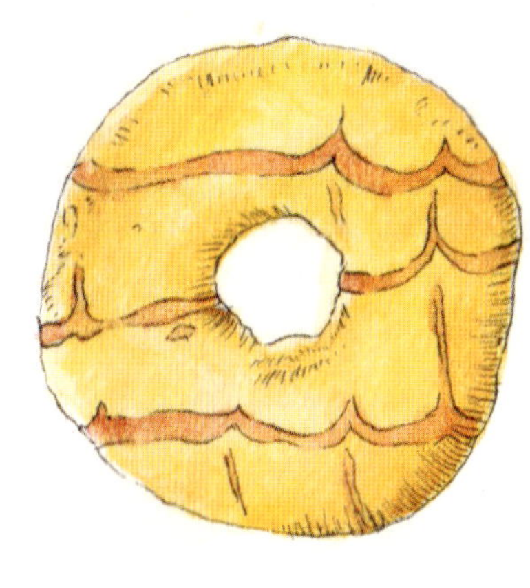

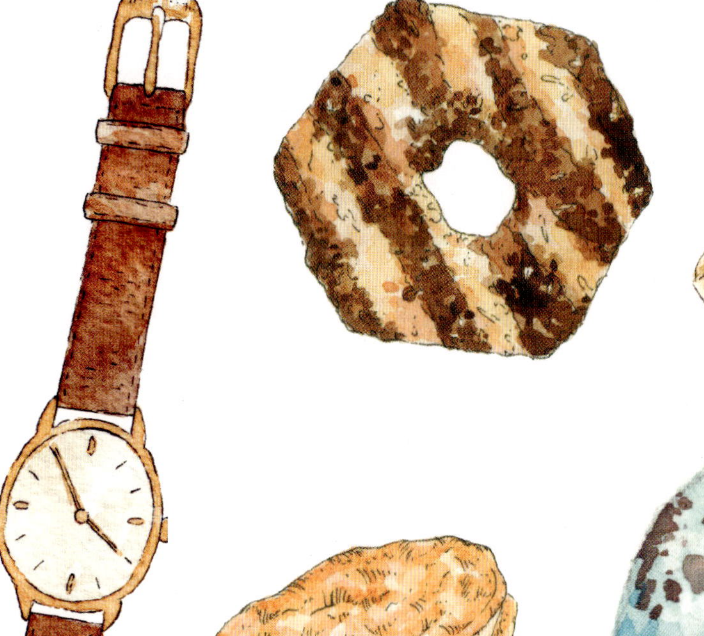

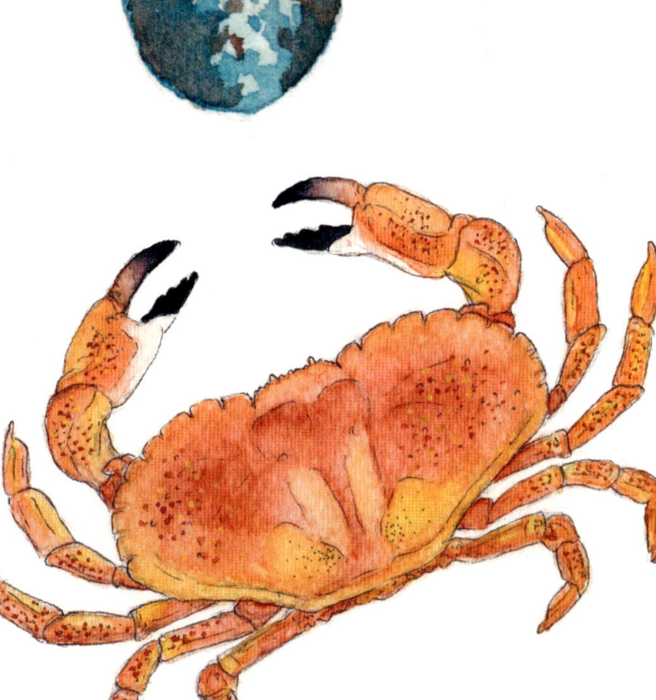

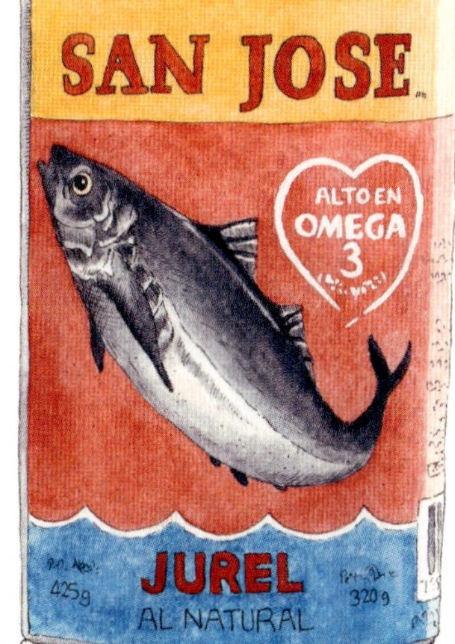

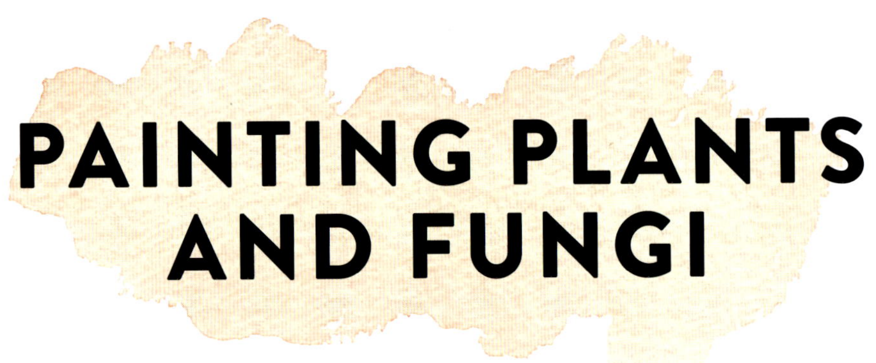

PAINTING PLANTS AND FUNGI

Three natural studies with which to build your skills

Plants and fungi make versatile subjects for painting, covering a wonderful variety of textures and shades. From houseplants to woodland mushrooms, there's no end to the inspiration here, and specimens are easily accessible on the whole.

Organic subjects are ideal for practising your skills. Soft edges and natural imperfections mean there's less pressure to strive for perfection and greater potential for recovering from mistakes.

46 PRICKLY CACTI

This exercise makes use of the bold layering demonstrated on pages 20–21. You'll also 'draw' using the paintbrush right from the start (see pages 10–11).

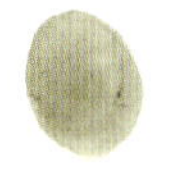

Sap Green

Green Gold

Perylene Green

Ultramarine Blue

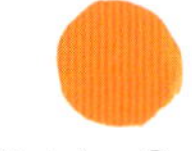

Cadmium Orange

1. Start by mixing several different shades of green by changing the amount of blue and yellow in each mix. If you have a turquoise in your palette, try using that, too, to get some really punchy colours.

2. Manipulate the paint to help you capture the shape of each cactus. Use just the tip of a fine brush to create points and apply more pressure to achieve the wider branches.

3. As you complete each layer, leave it to dry thoroughly so the colours don't run. This is especially important before adding the final bold details and cactus spikes.

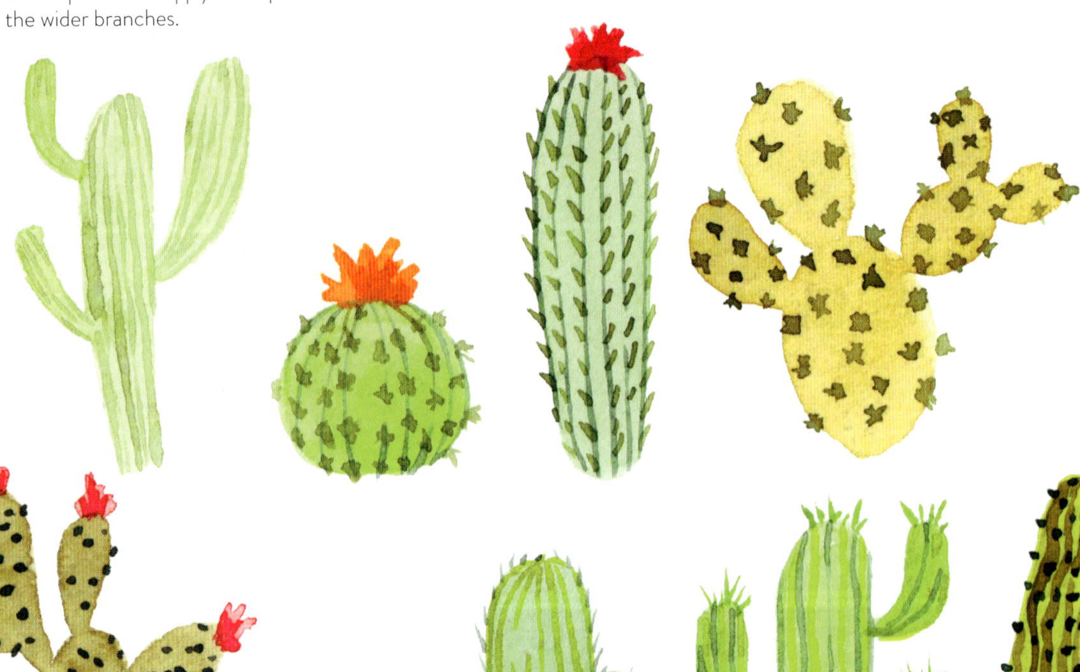

47 SUCCULENTS

Succulents are incredibly popular plants, filling window ledges in many homes and garden rockeries. They are very satisfying to paint due to their repeating patterns and charmingly organic shapes.

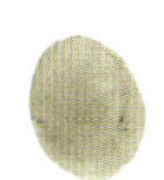

Sap Green

Green Gold

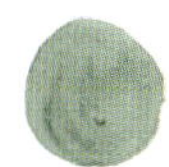

Perylene Green

1. If you want to make a precise painting, sketch the leaves out first using a pencil.
2. Go over your pencil sketch using a waterproof fine liner pen, adding fine texture and crosshatching where there would be shadows.
3. Rub away the pencil and begin your first layer of watercolour. Build several layers using the pulling techniques on pages 22–23.
4. Add the darkest layers where there are shadows, working wet-on-dry to blend any harsh edges.

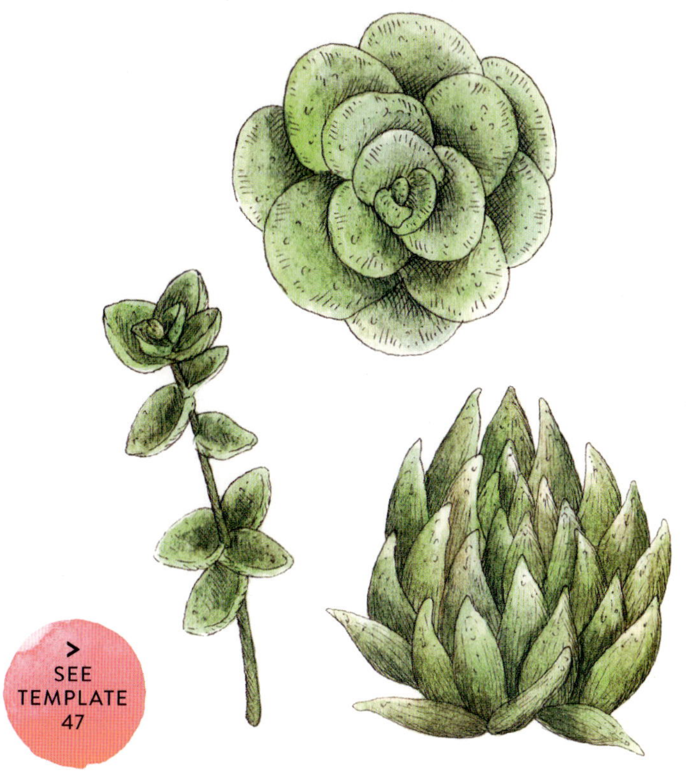

48 FAIRYTALE MUSHROOMS

This is a great exercise for using graphite and pen for the finer details, giving the finished fungi greater realism.

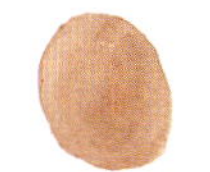

Vandyke Brown

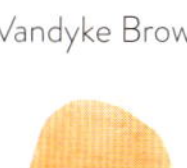

Deep Ochre

Indian Red

Alizarin Crimson

Yellow Ochre

1. Sketch each mushroom out using a pencil, paying particular attention to the finer details of their gills.
2. To create crisp lines around the white areas of the cap, draw haphazard areas first with pencil.
3. Fill in the cap using a brown-orange wash, while leaving the lighter areas unpainted.
4. To add finer detail, use a pen to draw fine black lines once the last wash has dried.

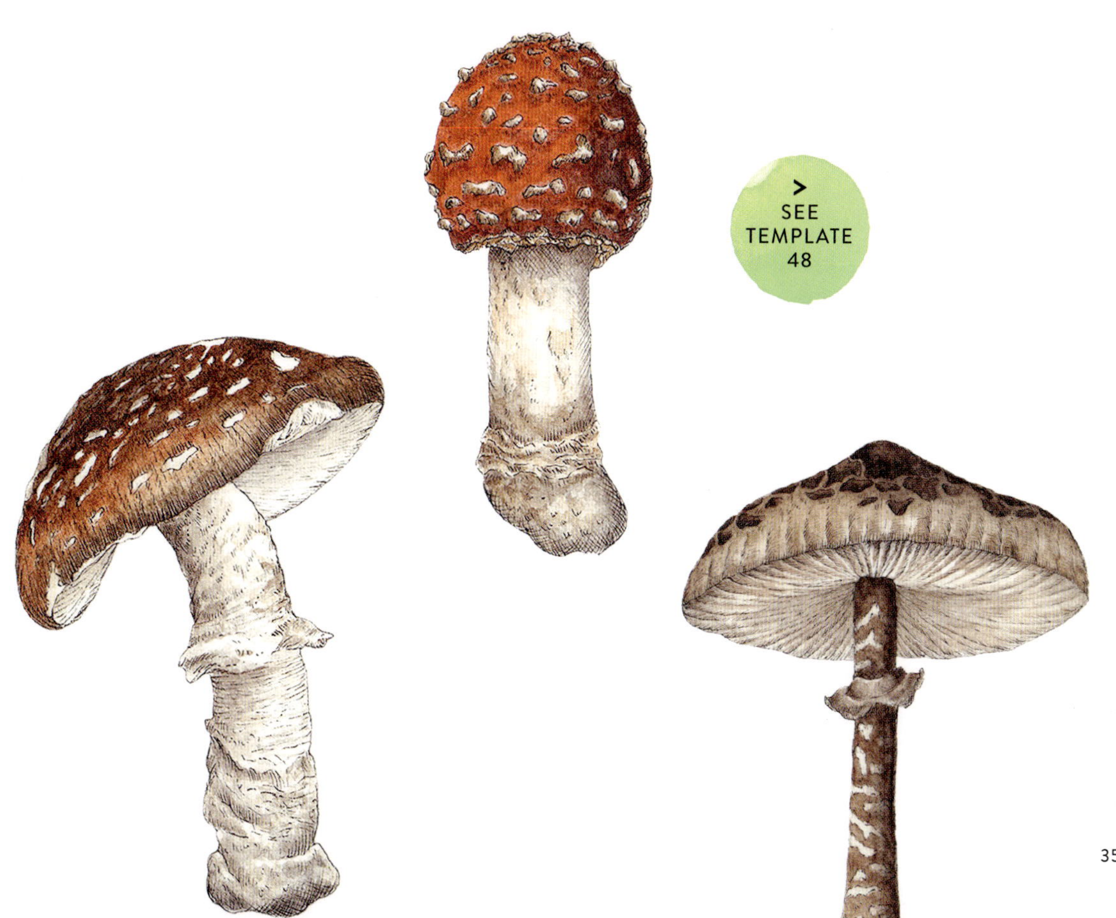

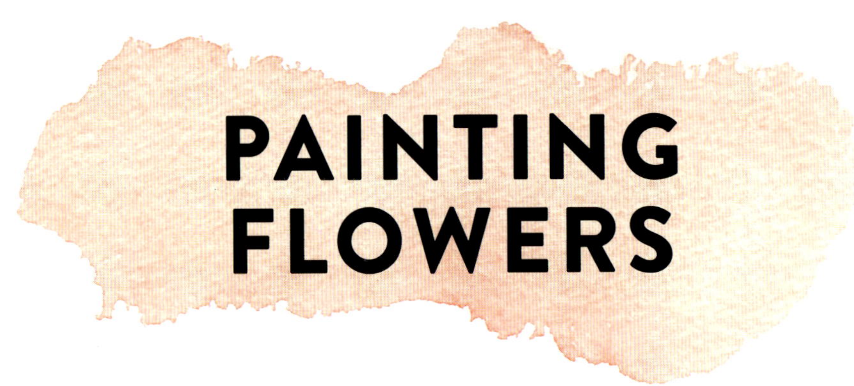

PAINTING FLOWERS

Three floral skills to put into practice

The delicate details of florals require a lighter touch than most other subjects. You need to keep your hand and wrist supple, while applying little pressure. The skill lies in building layers of colours very slowly using just the tip of the brush to render veins and shadows within the petals.

A relaxed hand is key here, as removing any the stiffness will let the brush glide smoothly across the paper.

49 SIMPLE PETALS

1. Start by painting the centre of the flower. Apply very little pressure as you create a series if interlocking c-shapes.

2. As you work out from the centre, continue to create the c-shapes, but allow them to grow thicker by applying more pressure. Finish with a row of thick c-shaped petals around the outermost edge.

3. Once the first layer of paint is dry, use a darker pigment to add accents here and there.

Alizarin Crimson

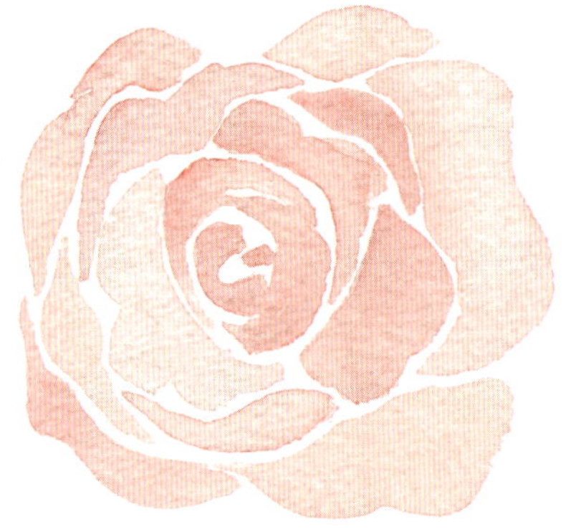

50 A DELICATE BLOOM

This pansy task offers a good opportunity to practise pulling colour (see page 22), as many varieties of this flower have a different coloured centre.

1. Start by painting the petals with a light wash and leave to dry.

2. Add a second colour to the centre of the flower and blend by pulling the colour towards the middle section of each petal.

3. Once this is dry, darken the very centre of the flower using a brush loaded with more pigment.

4. Paint the stem and a few leaves to finish it off.

Cobalt Teal

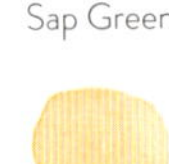

Sap Green

Yellow Ochre

Deep Ochre

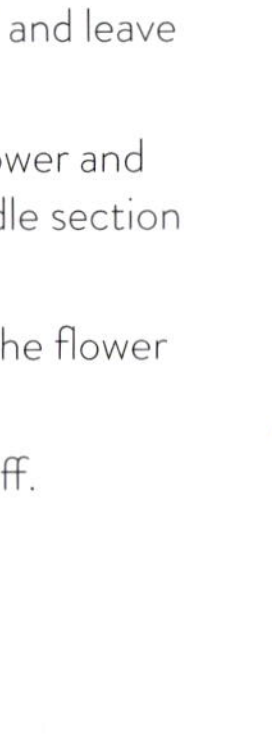

Green Gold

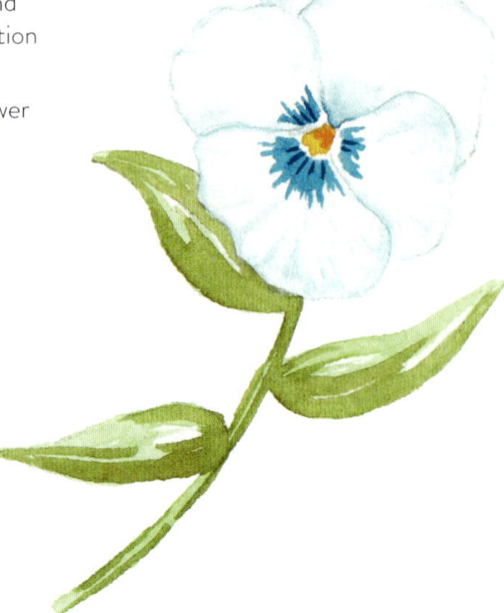

51

DETAILED FLOWERS

For botanical drawings such as this iris, watercolour gains more depth and becomes increasingly detailed with each layer you add. The method requires patience, as it invariably involves more layers. Use the techniques opposite to build each petal using three or four colours. Plan the highlights before you start and blend in darker colours by pulling the paint. Once the final layer is dry, you can add the finest details using the tip of your smallest paintbrush and light pressure.

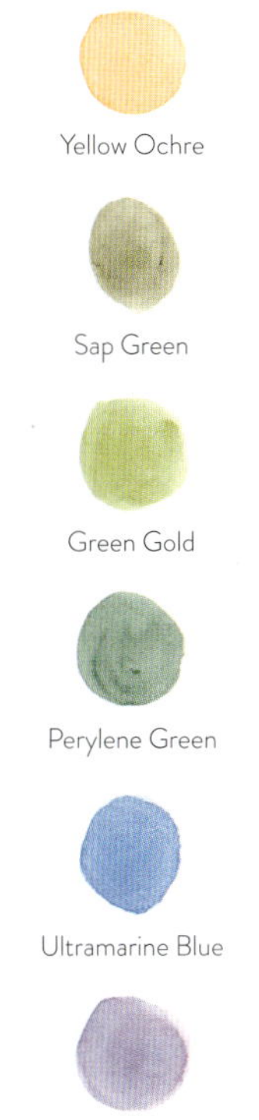

Yellow Ochre

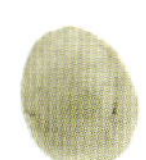

Sap Green

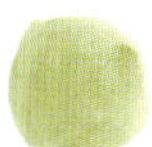

Green Gold

Perylene Green

Ultramarine Blue

Ultramarine Blue and
Pyrrol Crimson

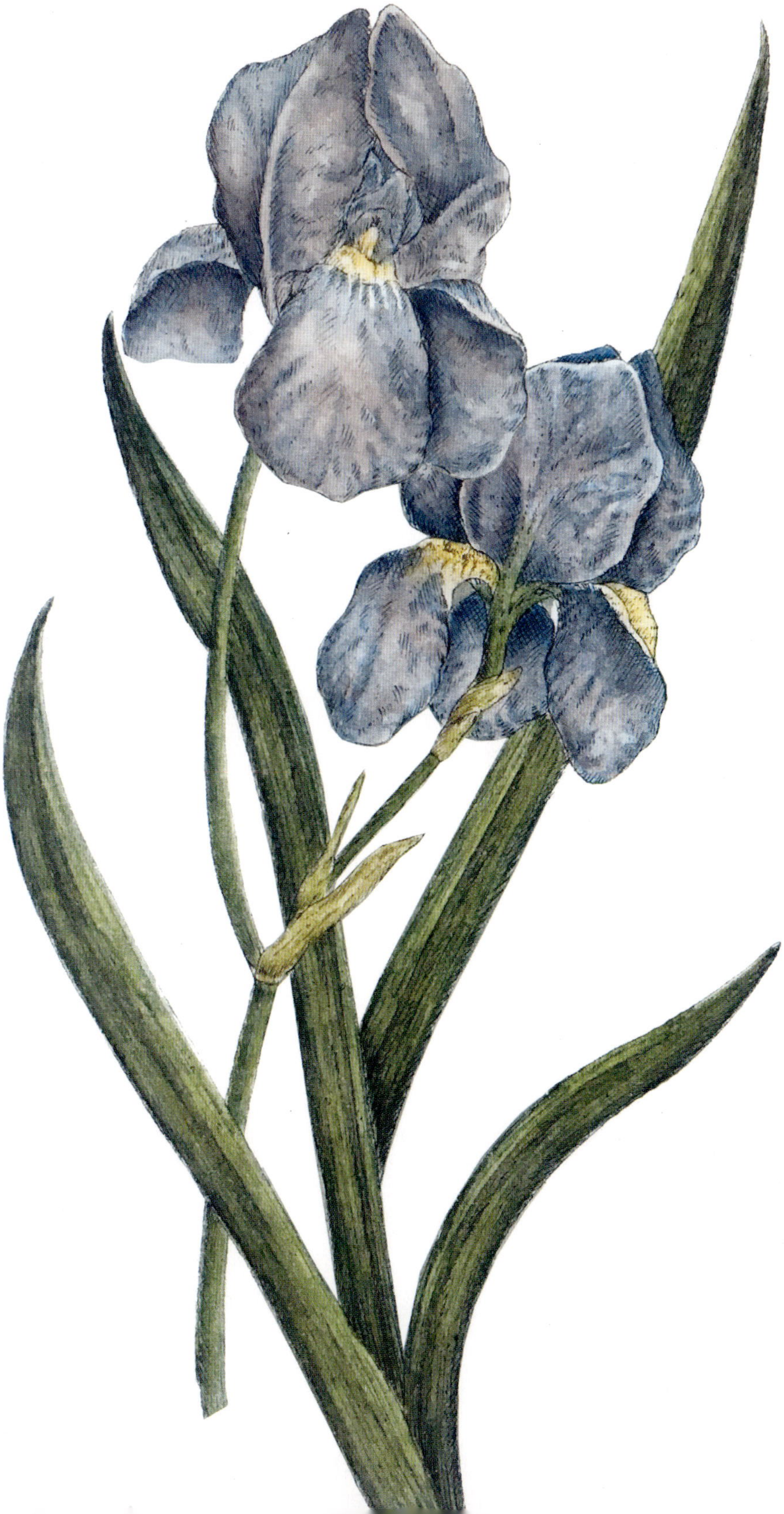

>
SEE
TEMPLATE
51

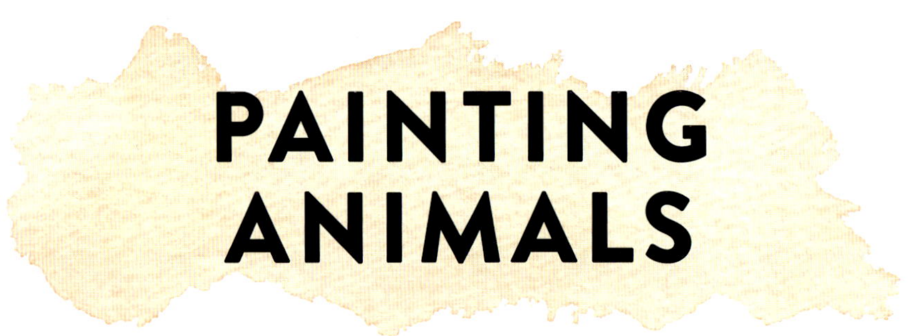

PAINTING ANIMALS

Four ways to master lifelike animal characteristics

When painting animals, the key to success lies not only in rendering realistic physical characteristics, but also in capturing movement. For the latter, you can work on a creature's stance and use well-placed shading to bring certain elements of the animal into the foreground for greater three-dimensionality. Tracing the animal's silhouette rather than applying the paint in vertical strokes adds more dynamism, too.

52 INSECTS

1. Sketch the outline of your bee.
2. Paint in the eye, using a shade of blue-grey.
3. Start to add the furry parts of the bee, starting with the black of the face, and allowing the black to blend a little into the yellow. Allowing the colours to smudge will make the bee look furrier.
4. You can use two shades of yellow here to create some highlights.
5. Using the tip of your finest brush and a lot of black pigment, add the legs and antennae.
6. For the wings, use a very watered down black or beige to define them, adding veins using just the tip of your brush.
7. Finally add some paint flecks around the bees to resemble pollen.

Cadmium Yellow

Yellow Ochre

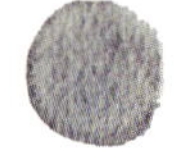

Deep Ochre

Payne's Grey

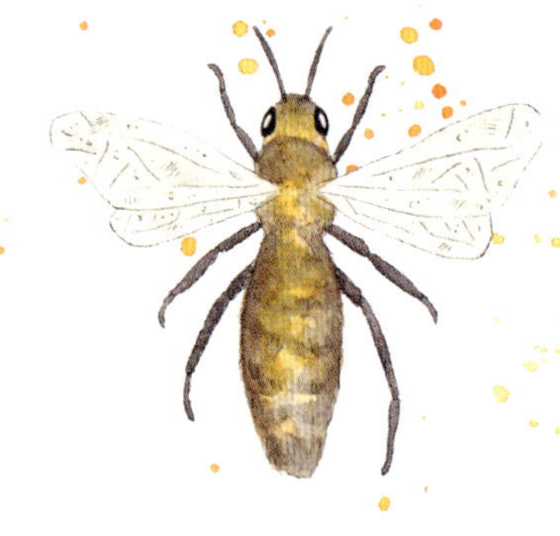
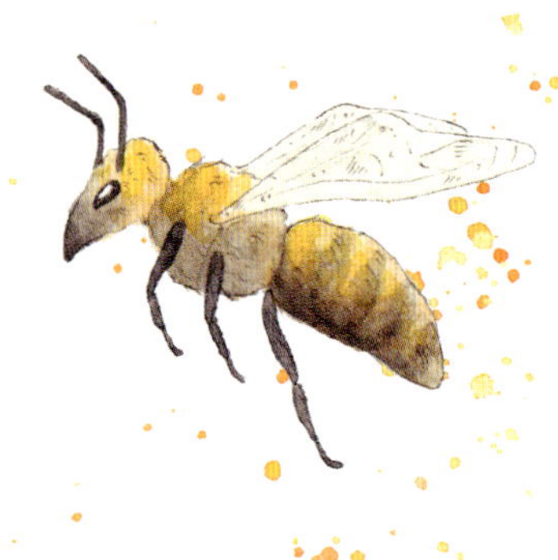

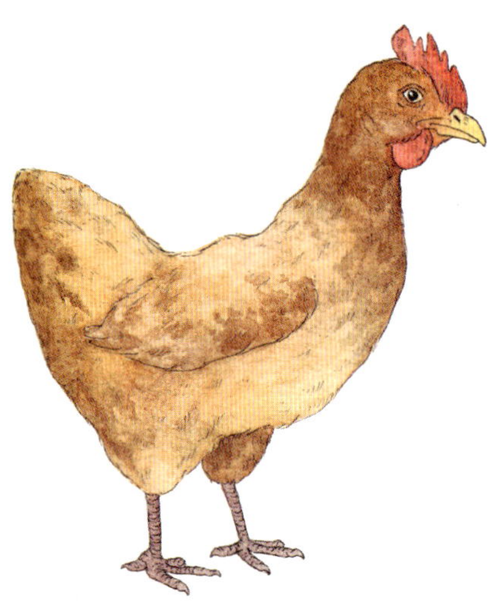

53 BIRDS

When painting birds or animals with striking fur, there is often a temptation to try to define every hair or feather, but this can have a strangely deadening effect. Instead, it is better to adopt a simple painting style to establish the general shape of the bird, and to add just a touch of definition.

Deep Ochre

1. Using a warm brown, establish the general shape of the bird.
2. Next, use a darker brown to give the form shape and dimension.
3. Now add the details, trying not to overdo them. You don't need to define every feather.
4. With a light touch of red, add the details of wattle and comb to its head.

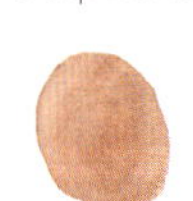

Vandyke Brown

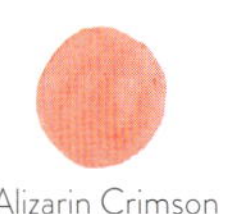

Alizarin Crimson

Ultramarine Blue and
Pyrrol Crimson

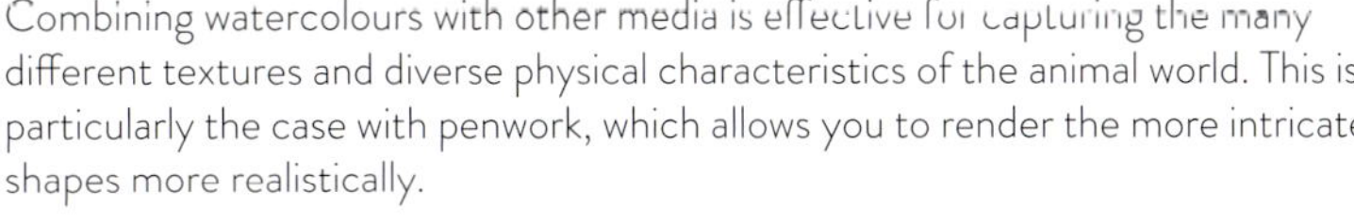

54 ANIMAL REALISM

Combining watercolours with other media is effective for capturing the many different textures and diverse physical characteristics of the animal world. This is particularly the case with penwork, which allows you to render the more intricate shapes more realistically.

Pyrrol Crimson

1. Use a waterproof fine liner pen to create the outline of your creature – in this case an octopus. Really focus on the shapes that define the creature – for example, the twists and turns of the octopus's tentacles.

2. Once you have built several layers of colour, you can add shadows and texture using the crosshatching and stippling techniques described on page 31 to emphasize the suckers.

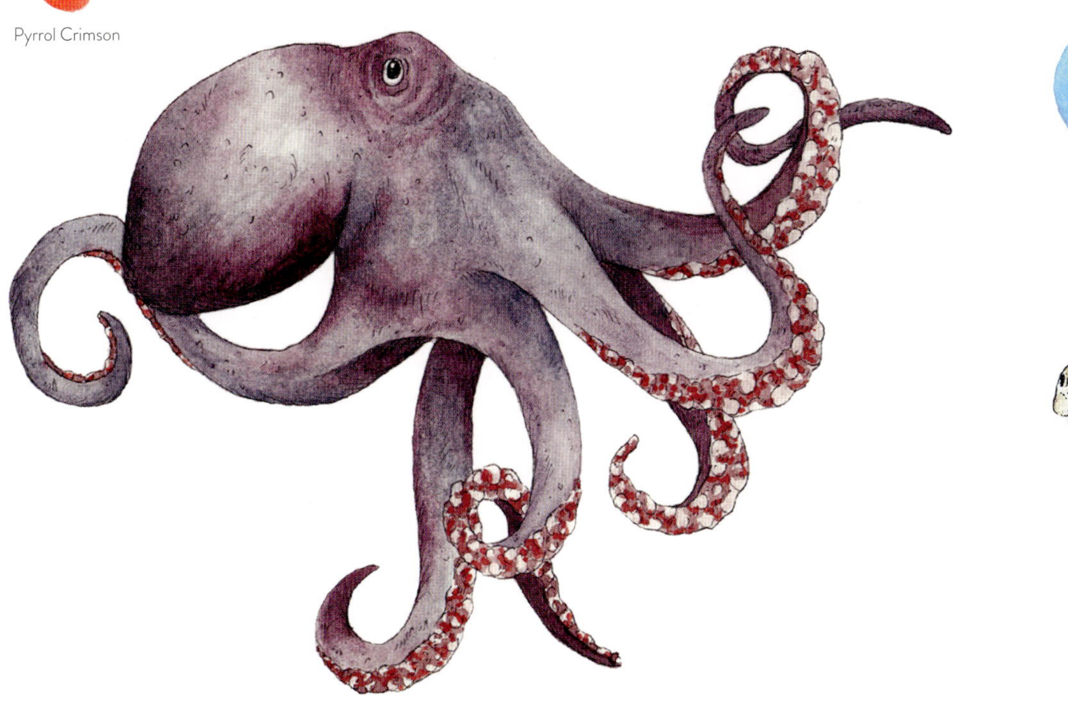

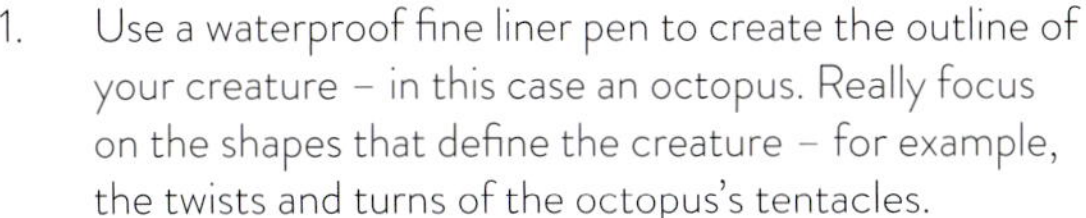

55 SKIN AND HIDE

Many animals have skin or fur with intricate patterning. The key to painting such things as spots or stripes is to recognize the fact that these features do not lie flat against the animal, but follow the natural lines of its body. So, the stripes of a zebra would not be perfectly vertical, but would curve slightly around the zebra's stomach. In the case of a giraffe, the spots may be very small around the face and much larger on the body area. Smaller spots tend to be dense and their shapes become distorted as they wrap around a leg or shoulder. The best way to render spots and stripes is to use glazing and pulling techniques to build colour initially (see pages 20–23), and then to make the spots stand out using more pigment and less water.

Cadmium Yellow

Yellow Ochre

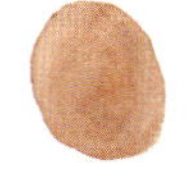

Vandyke Brown

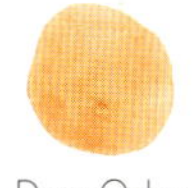

Deep Ochre

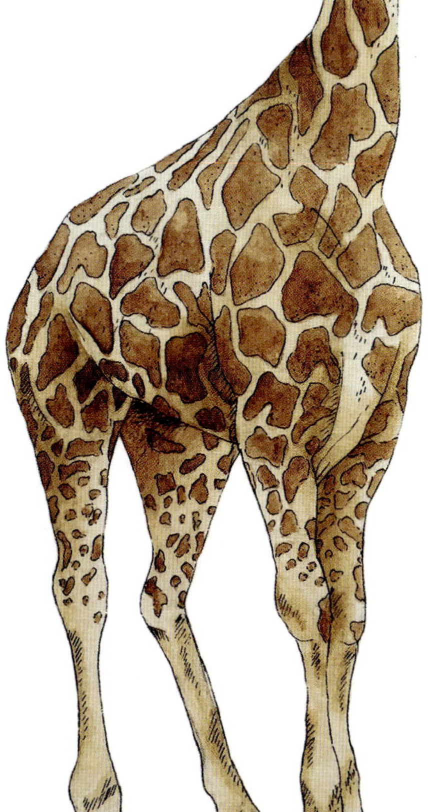

PAINTING FOOD

Three studies for painting realistic food

While many subjects are rendered using soft gradients and smooth blending, foods often involve effects that create texture. Base washes may be perfectly blended, but it's the finer details that will make food leap off the page.

Different textures require different brushstrokes – wide, overlapping strokes for jam and jelly, small c-shapes made with the tip of a brush for the little flecks in baked goods, and tiny dabs for seeds and sprinkles, for example. Changing the direction of your brushstrokes now and again will add an extra dimension.

56 PACKAGING

When it comes to food packaging, things don't get more colourful and inventive than sweet wrappers. Sweets come in so many forms that painting a bag of pick-n-mix can be great practice for a range of different watercolour techniques. For hard sweets think about using the highlight effects on page 25 to show bright reflections. For fizzy sweets use the tip of the brush to create a stipple effect for the sugar crystals.

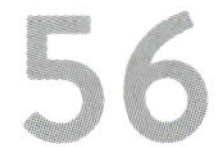

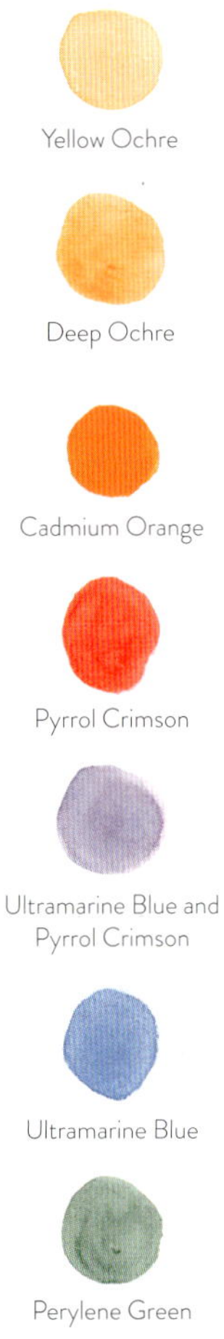

Yellow Ochre

Deep Ochre

Cadmium Orange

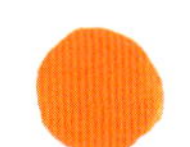

Pyrrol Crimson

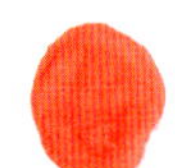

Ultramarine Blue and Pyrrol Crimson

Ultramarine Blue

Perylene Green

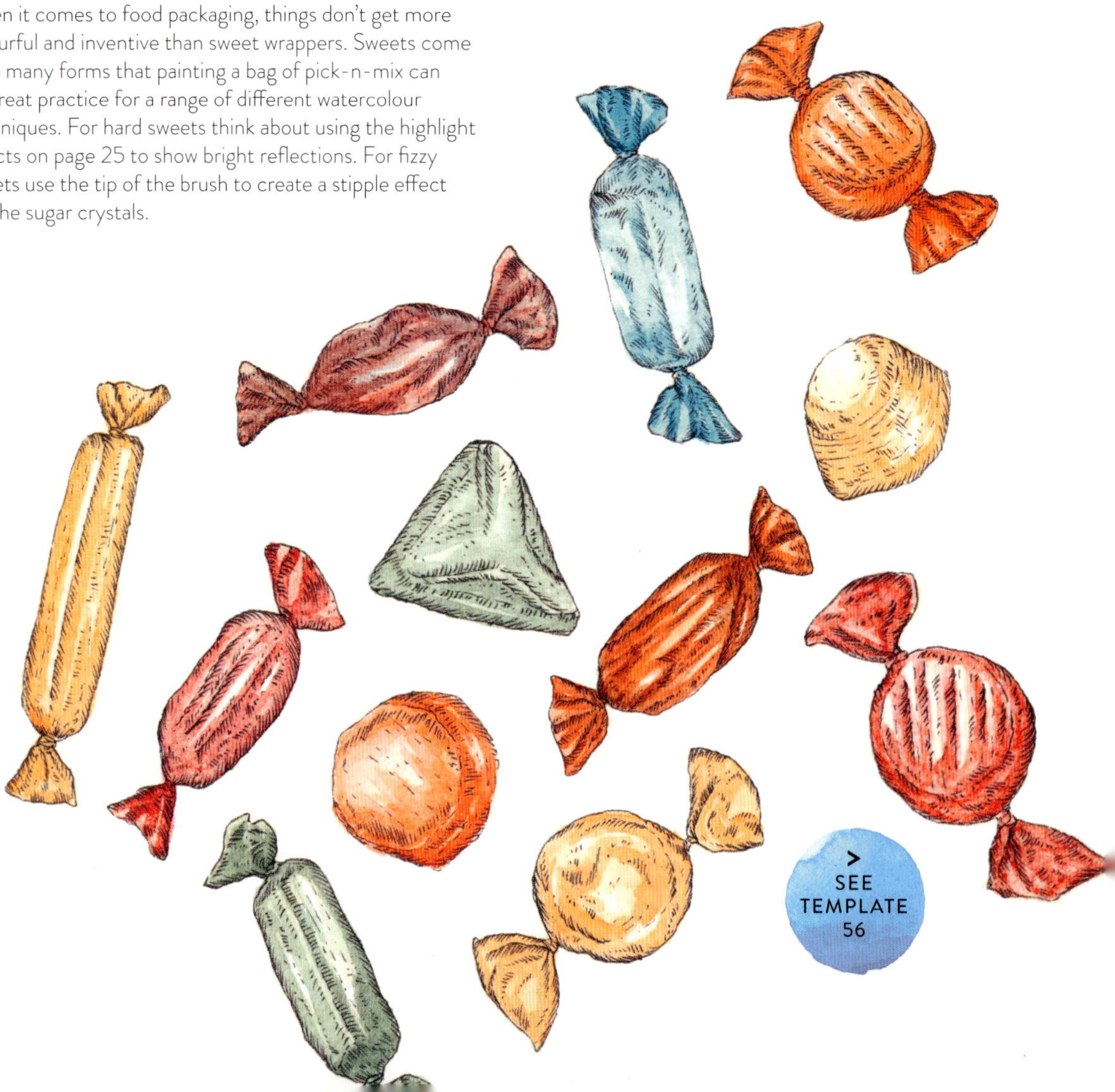

> SEE TEMPLATE 56

57   BAKED GOODS

There's something very satisfying about painting a subject with a super crumbly texture. Cookies, cakes and crusty bread are all good subjects here, making use of the glazing and pulling techniques on pages 20–23.

1. Once you have the basic shape of your baked goods – in this case a cookie – use a few light washes to mark out areas of highlight and shadow.
2. Start to build texture across the cookie using just the tip of the brush.
3. Once dry, add a darker shade to emphasize some of these areas a little more – cracks in the surface or a particularly crispy ridge, for example.
4. Finish with an even darker shade, used sparingly, to create the chocolate chips.

Cadmium Yellow

Yellow Ochre

Vandyke Brown

Deep Ochre

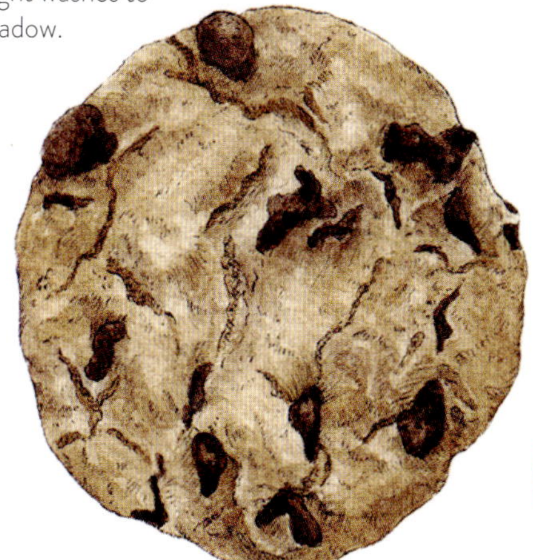

58   WHAT'S ON YOUR PLATE?

If you're stuck for subject matter, just paint what's on your plate. Most meals include a variety of textured foods, allowing you to call on a mix of paint techniques. Burgers in buns and sandwiches present the ideal challenge in this respect.

1. Each layer of a hamburger has a different texture, so make sure to vary your brushstrokes for each stage.
2. Starting with the burger itself, build up the washes and show the indentations of the meat using slight dabs of the brush.
3. Lettuce and tomato have smoother textures, best rendered using wider and bigger brush marks.
4. The bun requires the least amount of detail. Use glazing techniques to build up rich colour and then use the tip of your finest brush to add seeds to the top of the bun.

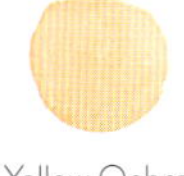

Yellow Ochre

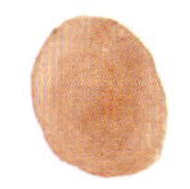

Vandyke Brown

Deep Ochre

Ultramarine Blue and
Pyrrol Crimson

Green Gold

Perylene Green

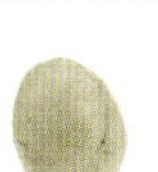

Sap Green

Alizarin Crimson

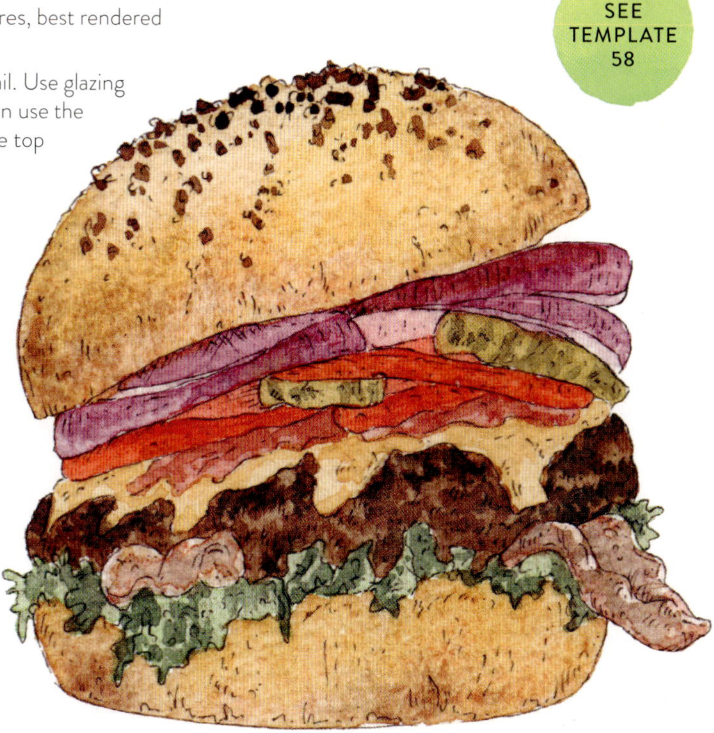

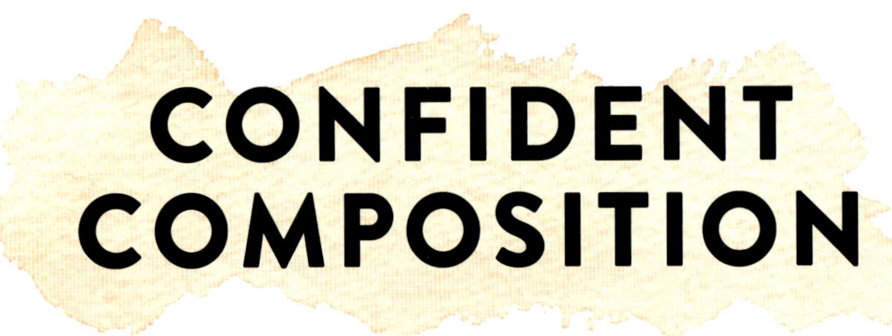

CONFIDENT COMPOSITION

Four steps to creating better compositions

How you position shapes on paper is crucial for balance in a painting. Placing the subject centrally usually makes sense, but giving it an interesting crop or placing it off-centre can be more interesting visually.

Whatever you opt for, there are a number of key considerations. Firstly, you need to balance the positive and negative space – too much negative space will make your painting look empty and unfinished. Too little negative space willl make it tight and busy. Confident composition is something that builds with practice. Once you get it right, it will make a painting feel 'complete' and polished while also telling a story.

59 THOUGHTFUL COLOUR CHOICES

When planning a composition, your colour choices should always be at the forefront of your mind. Revisit the sections on colour theory (see pages 6–7) and create little swatches of colours that you plan to use before you start. See how they sit next to each other on paper.

>
SEE
TEMPLATE
60

60 CROPPING

Cropping is key. Think about how a crop can alter the dimensions of a painting. The bottom of a cliff cropped at the top left-hand corner with a rock pool going off the page really draws your eye to the coastline, pulling you into a story. Paint a similar scene with a strong crop that cuts through the painting.

Ultramarine Blue

Cobalt Teal

Payne's Grey

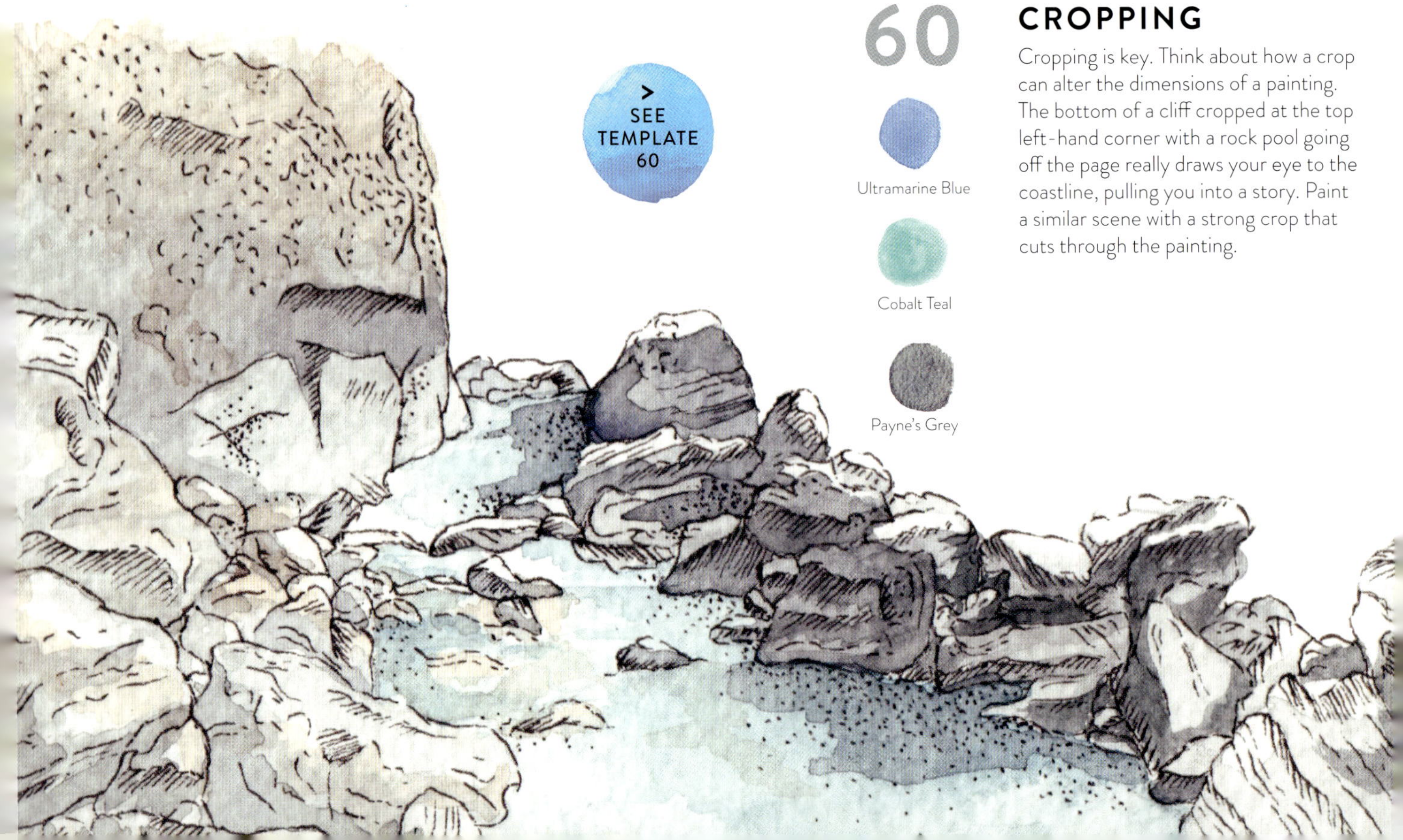

61 PLACEMENT

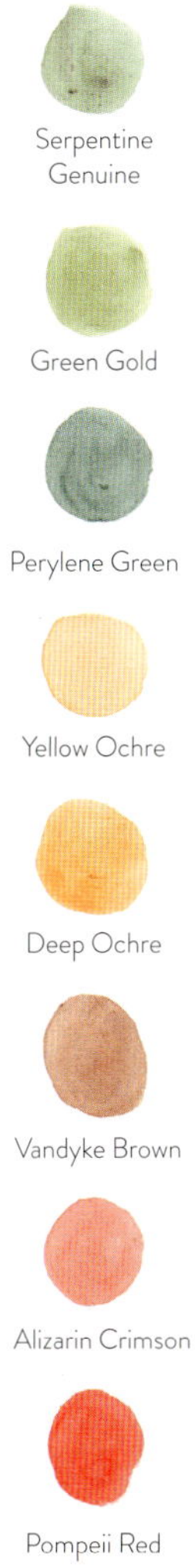

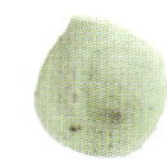

Serpentine
Genuine

Green Gold

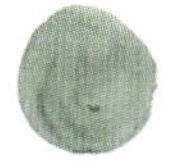

Perylene Green

Yellow Ochre

Deep Ochre

Vandyke Brown

Alizarin Crimson

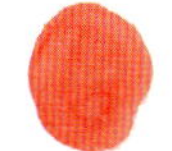

Pompeii Red

The placement of your subject matter will have an influence on your composition whether you have just one single object or a whole pattern to create. Here's a formula worth following to get a feel for it.

1. Paint three or five floral motifs of varying size. Space them out across the paper with adequate space for more elements between them.

2. Begin to fill these spaces with more flowers of varying size with equal spacing between them.

3. You will be left with a page full of flowers, perfectly spaced and forming a loose pattern.

> SEE TEMPLATE 61

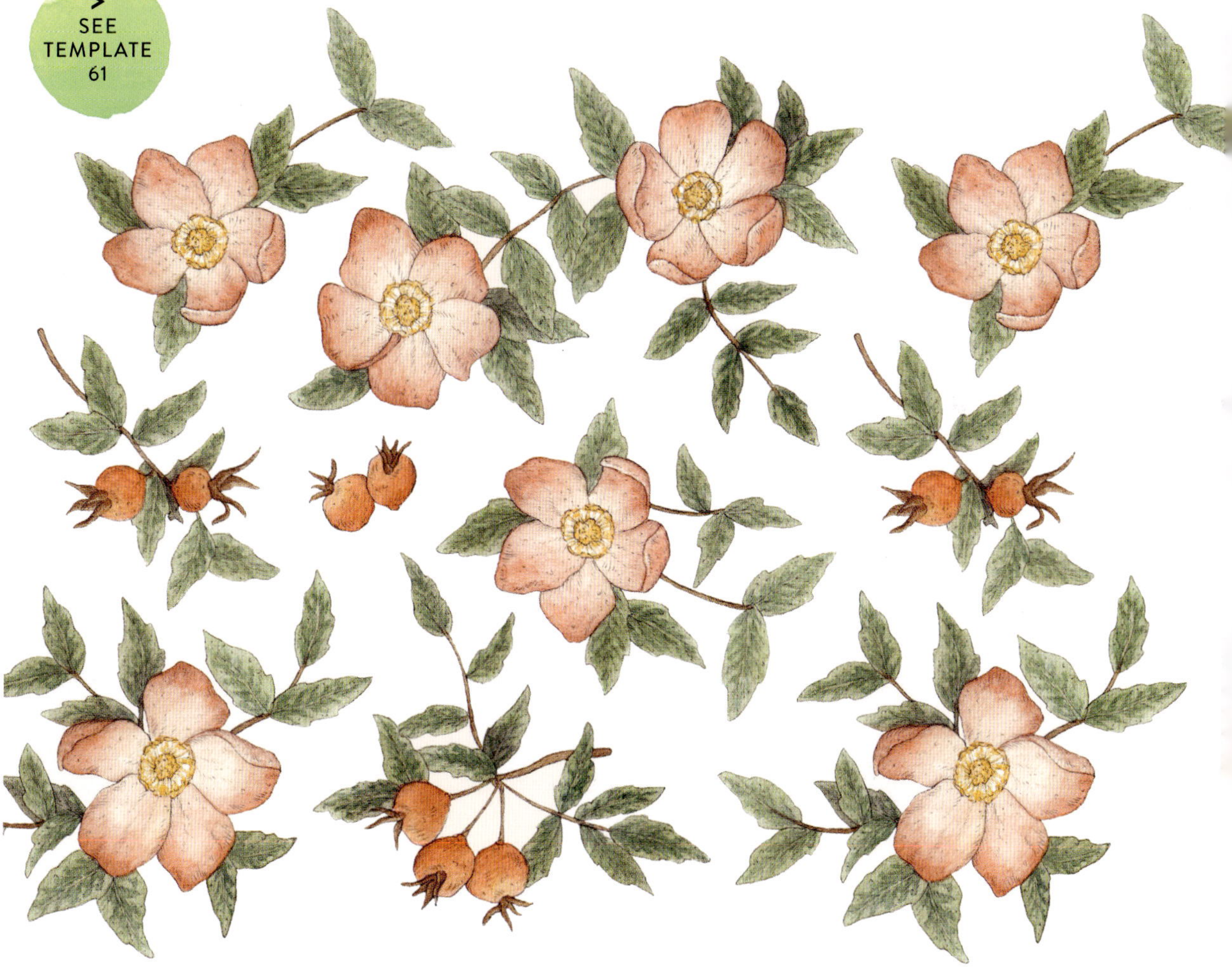

62 DISTRACTING ELEMENTS

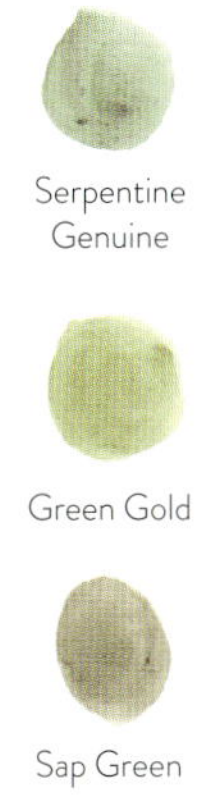

Serpentine
Genuine

Green Gold

Sap Green

It's all too easy for a painting to become very busy. Trying to fill the paper with detail makes it hard to settle on a focal point and tends to flatten a piece. One way to overcome this is to think about the relationship between foreground and background. For example, sketch out lots of tall grasses and wildflowers to create a meadow. Paint the grasses in the foreground with crisper lines and more detail, while using looser brushstrokes and much less detail for the background. Instantly you will have created a painting with depth and a clear focal point in the foreground, as the meadow recedes into the distance.

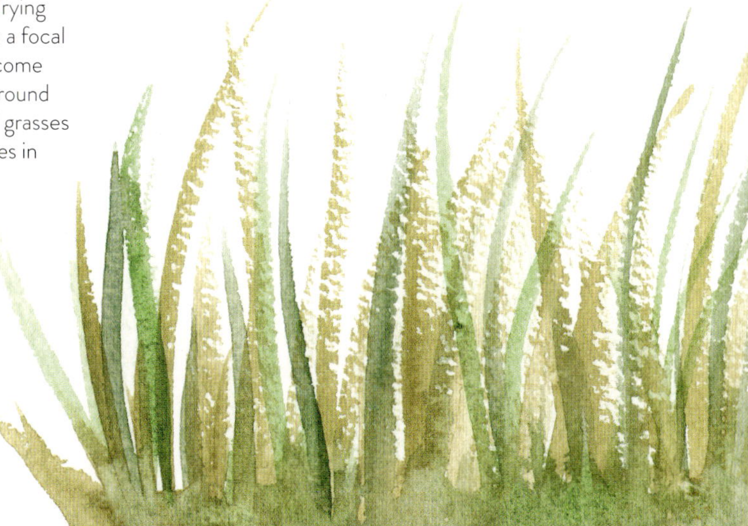

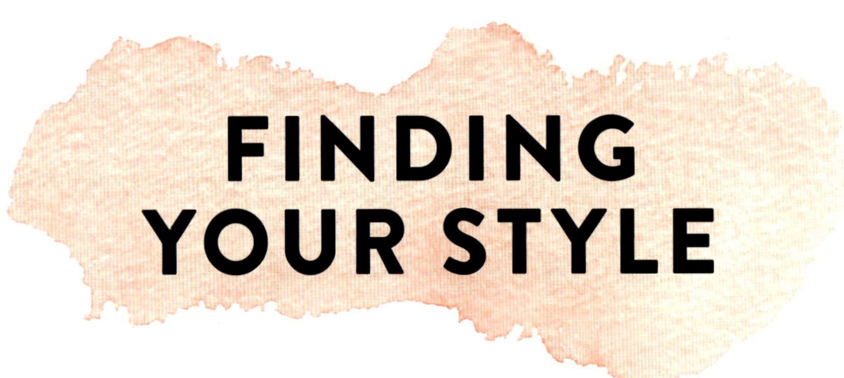

Three ways in which to develop your style

While learning to paint with watercolours, you will start to develop your own style. You'll pick up different techniques and will find yourself painting in the manner in which you are most comfortable. It will become your signature style and an extension of who you are.

You may reference other artists' work to discover new methods, but you'll always have a clear vision of what you want to create. You will see this when you use the templates in this book. Your work will differ from the examples next to each exercise, depending on your own personal preferences and application of the techniques.

63 PRACTISE

You will have heard this before, but practice really is key. Every artist does it each time they paint. It's simply a matter of knowing that the more you paint, the better your skills will become. No matter where you are on your artistic journey, practising will always help you improve. Try picking one subject and repaint it several times to gain confidence in its shape.

Ultramarine Blue

Yellow Ochre

Deep Ochre

Vandyke Brown

Alizarin Crimson

Ultramarine Blue and
Pyrrol Crimson

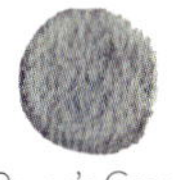

Payne's Grey

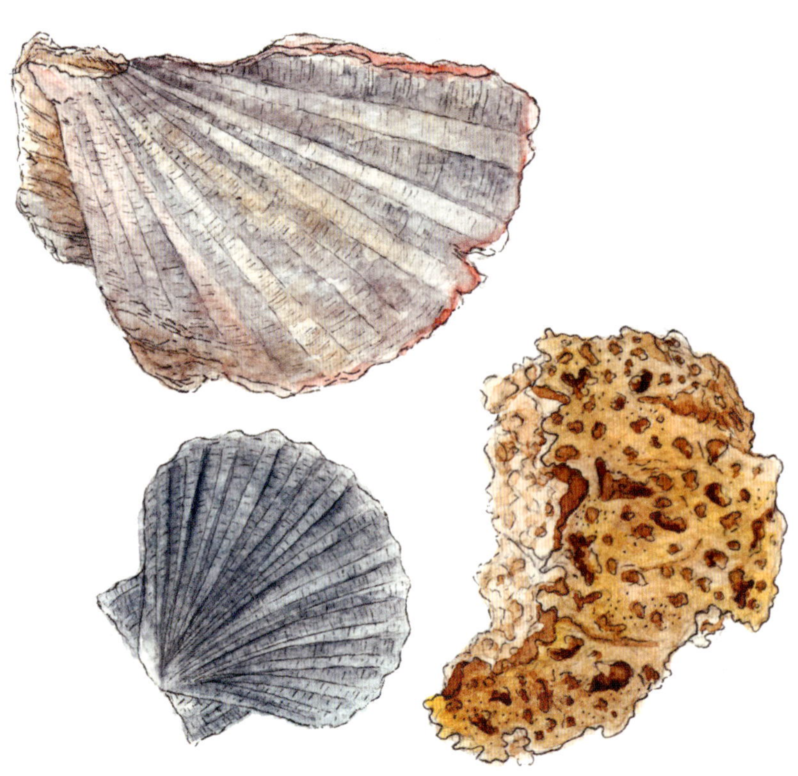

64

PAINT WITH CHARACTER

Vandyke Brown

Ultramarine Blue and
Pyrrol Crimson

Let your personality show through in your painting. If you're a little messy, don't force your painting to be perfect. If you tend towards the humorous, don't paint in a serious style when a comic-book style may suit you better. Try painting household items and use them to develop your style. One fun approach is to paint an armchair that represents you. It could be pristine and beautifully buttoned or perhaps the filling is falling out a little and there's one too many coffee stains. Try the same exercise with different objects – a jumper, a shrub or perhaps your favourite pudding.

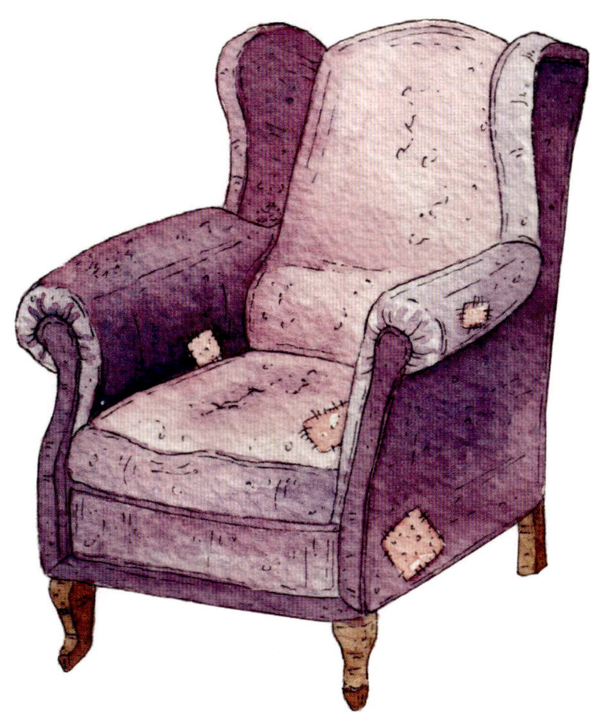

65

CONSTRUCTIVE CRITICISM

Cobalt Teal

Ultramarine Blue

Sap Green

Serpentine
Genuine

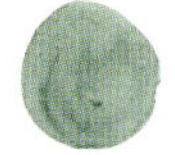

Perylene Green

Green Gold

Always be open to constructive criticism. There's something so personal about painting; what you create feels like an extension of yourself and by sharing what you paint, you physically put yourself out there. While criticism is never fun to hear, don't let it dishearten you. Sometimes comments can be useful.

Here is a useful exercise: try creating two paintings of the same type of subject – perhaps the plants you have in your home – a week apart. Lay the paintings alongside each other and see how you tackled each one differently. Think about the areas you like best and would like to replicate next time around.

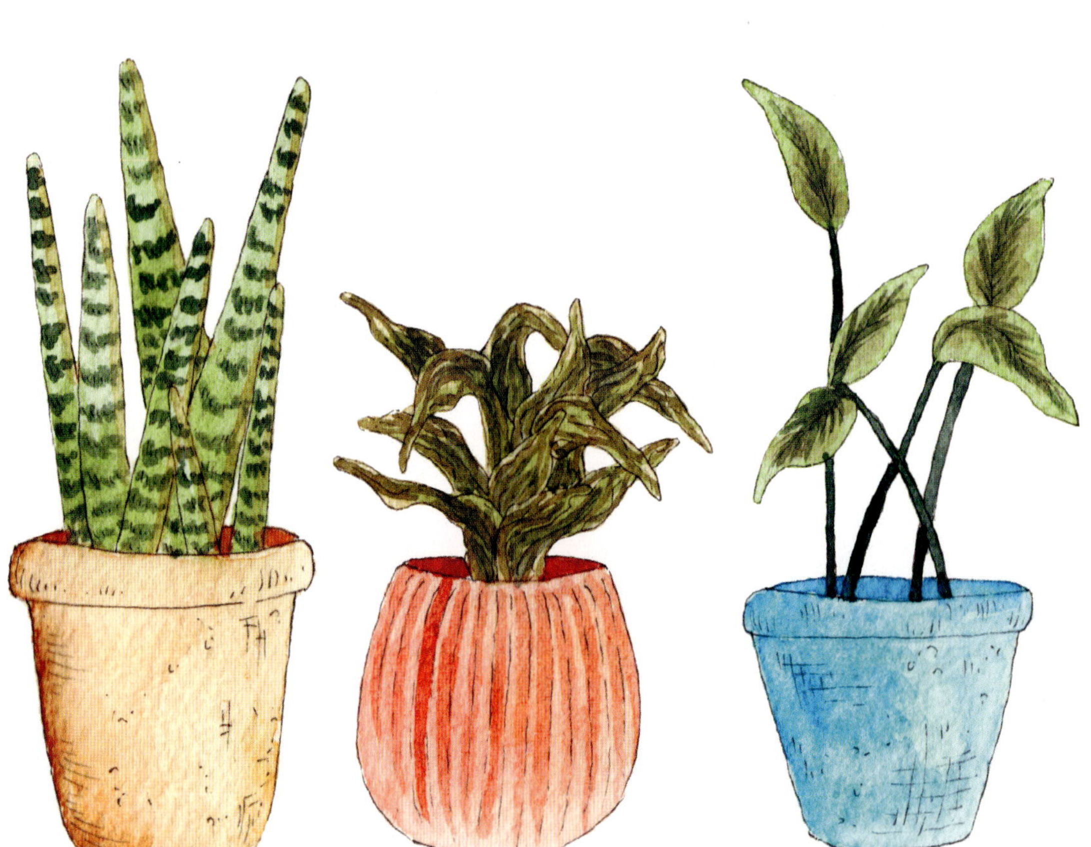

GET CREATIVE

Three ways to shake things up

Creativity doesn't always come naturally, but everyone can be creative in one way or another. Sometimes it helps to have a nudge in the right direction. Although the word 'creativity' has many interpretations, it mostly involves challenging yourself to think differently, perhaps in ways that you're not used to. Thinking creatively can be a great help when painting.

If you're struggling to think outside the box, then change the box! Change your environment, meet new people and try new things.

66 BE RESOURCEFUL

It is often much better to use what you have around you than to spend money on new materials that you may not even enjoy using. You'll also find it easier to get the creative juices flowing if you limit yourself. For example, instead of splashing out on a watercolour palette with 96 paints, stick to a small travel-sized one. You'll be surprised how much easier it is to paint when you have less choice. Challenge yourself to go back to the very beginning. Select just one colour and use all the painting techniques covered in this book to create a beautiful work of art.

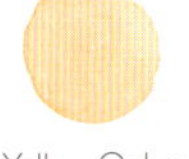

Yellow Ochre

Deep Ochre

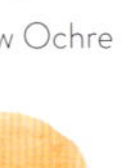

Vandyke Brown

Payne's Grey

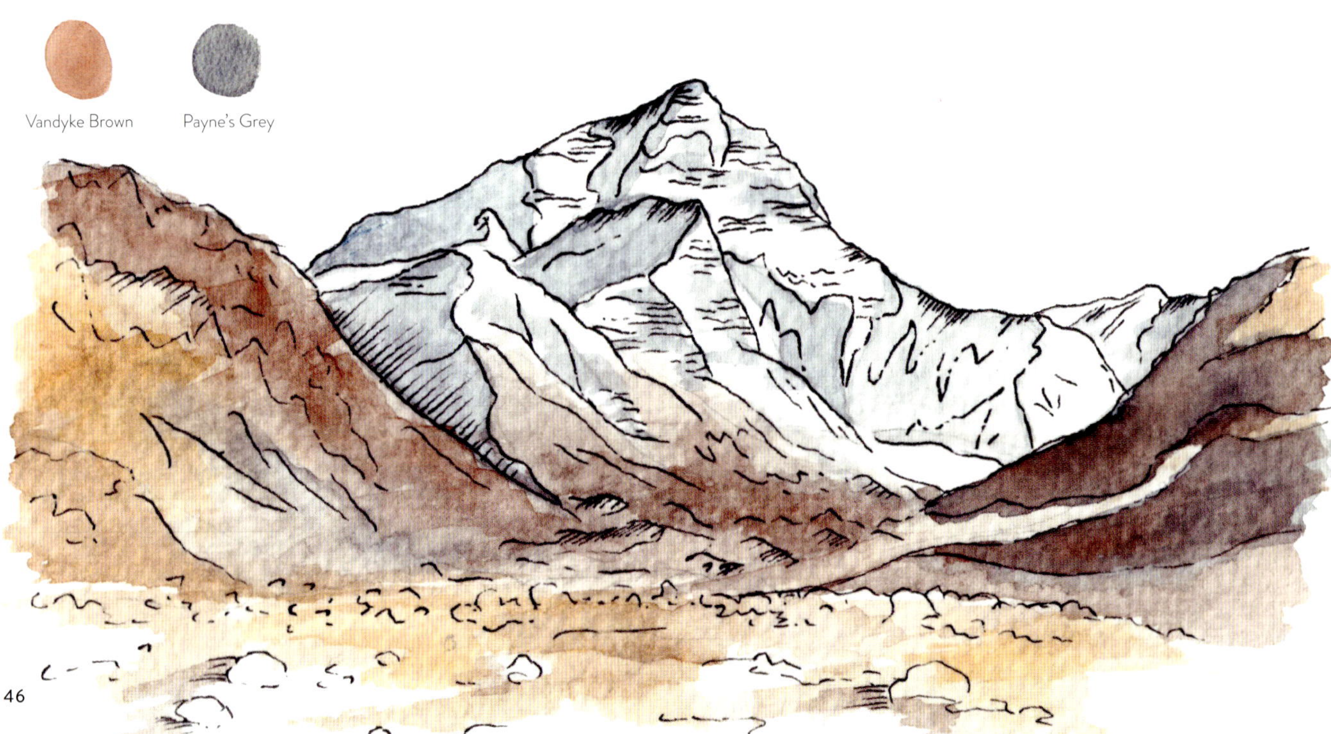

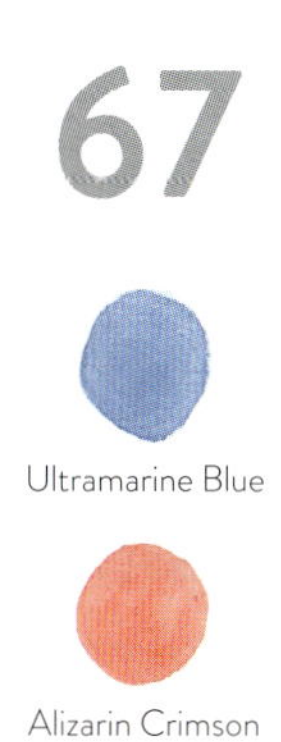

67 PAINT ANYWHERE INDOORS

Always be on the lookout for inspiration. If you've run off to a coffee shop, why not paint a still life while you are there. Still-life painting doesn't have to be boring and serious – you can paint anything you like, in any style you choose. Arrange coffee cup, sweet treats and cutlery on the table and paint the composition you've arranged.

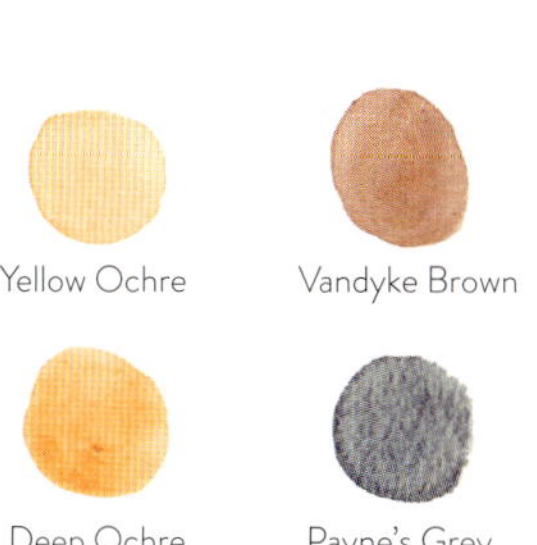

Ultramarine Blue

Alizarin Crimson

Pompeii Red

Yellow Ochre

Vandyke Brown

Indian Red

Deep Ochre

Payne's Grey

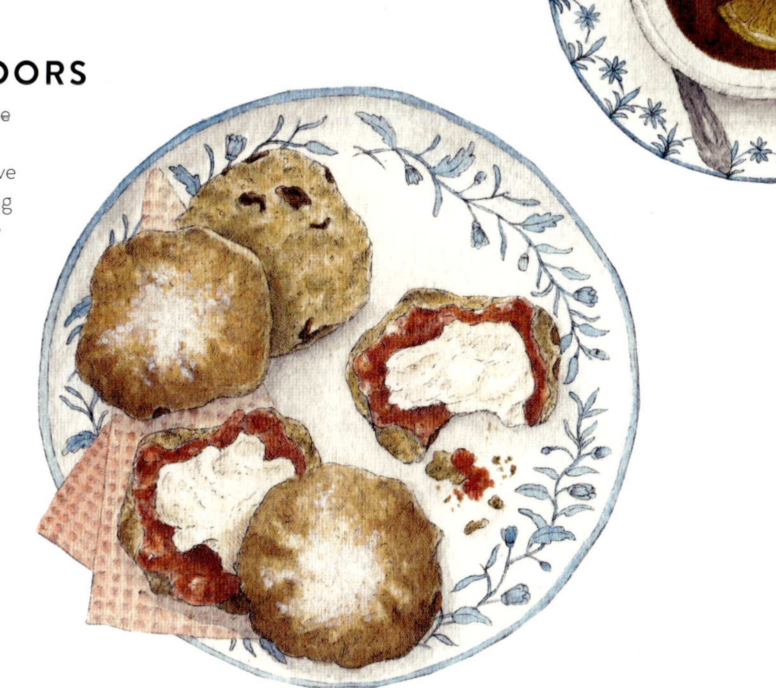

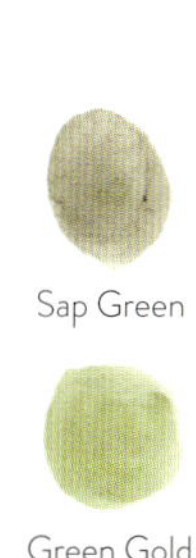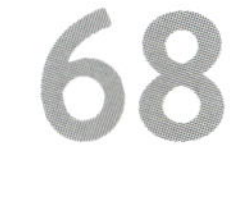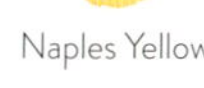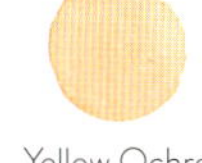

68 PAINT ANYWHERE OUTDOORS

It's surprisingly easy to find other people who also enjoy painting and drawing in their free time. Feel confident in talking about your new hobby – for all you know a co-worker may have recently picked up a paint brush for the first time. Be brave and share your paintings on social media. There are wonderfully supportive creative communities on Instagram. Look out for local 'sketch meetups.' Most cities host them and groups of up to 30 budding artists (both amateur and professional) meet up to paint outdoors together. In the meantime why not try painting outdoors by yourself? Take your palette and a jug of water out into the garden or your local park. You might notice how your painting style relaxes when you are enjoying being outdoors.

Sap Green

Green Gold

Perylene Green

Serpentine Genuine

Naples Yellow

Yellow Ochre

Indian Red

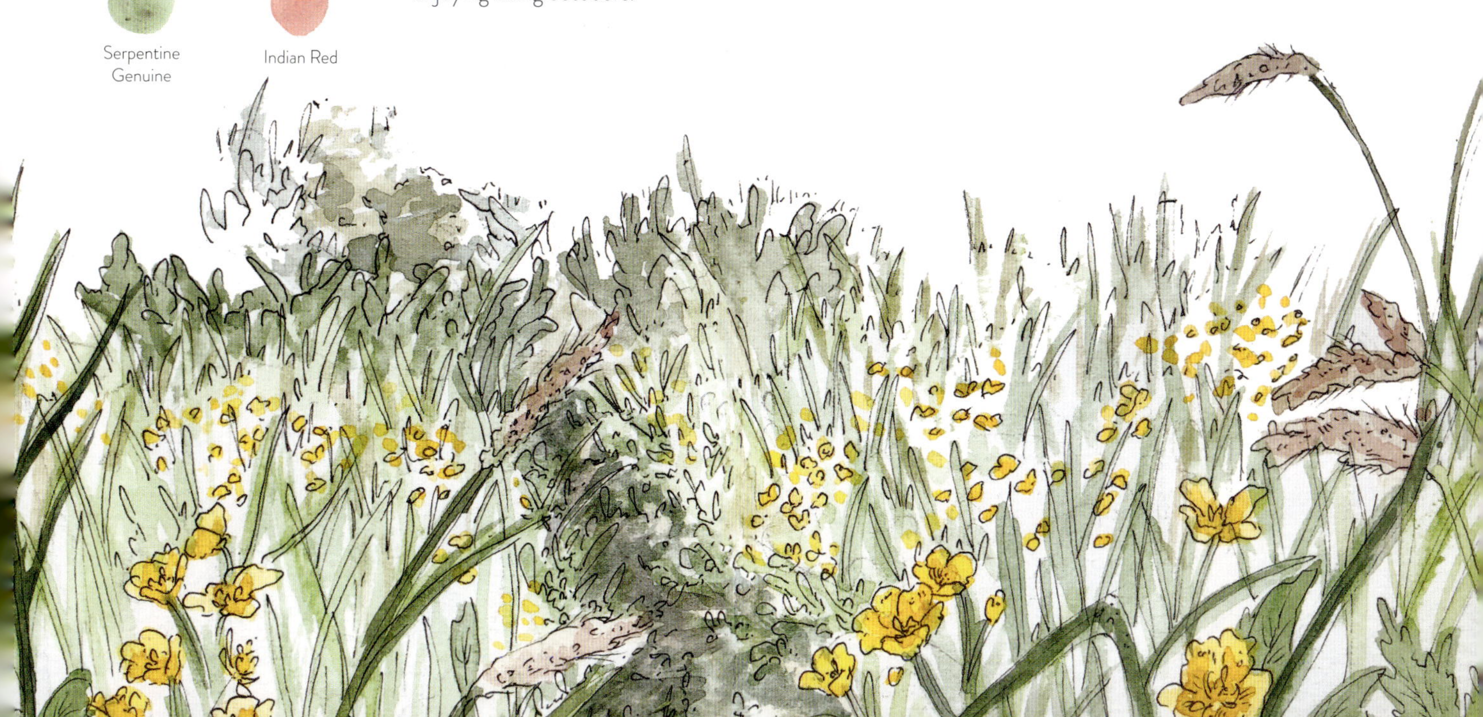

THE TEMPLATES

1 THE COLOUR WHEEL
Practise adding layers of colour (page 6). Make sure you clean your brush thoroughly to avoid creating unwanted shades.

Practise creating simple shapes (page 10). Use the shape of the paintbrush to help you and rotate the page where necessary so that your hand is comfortable.

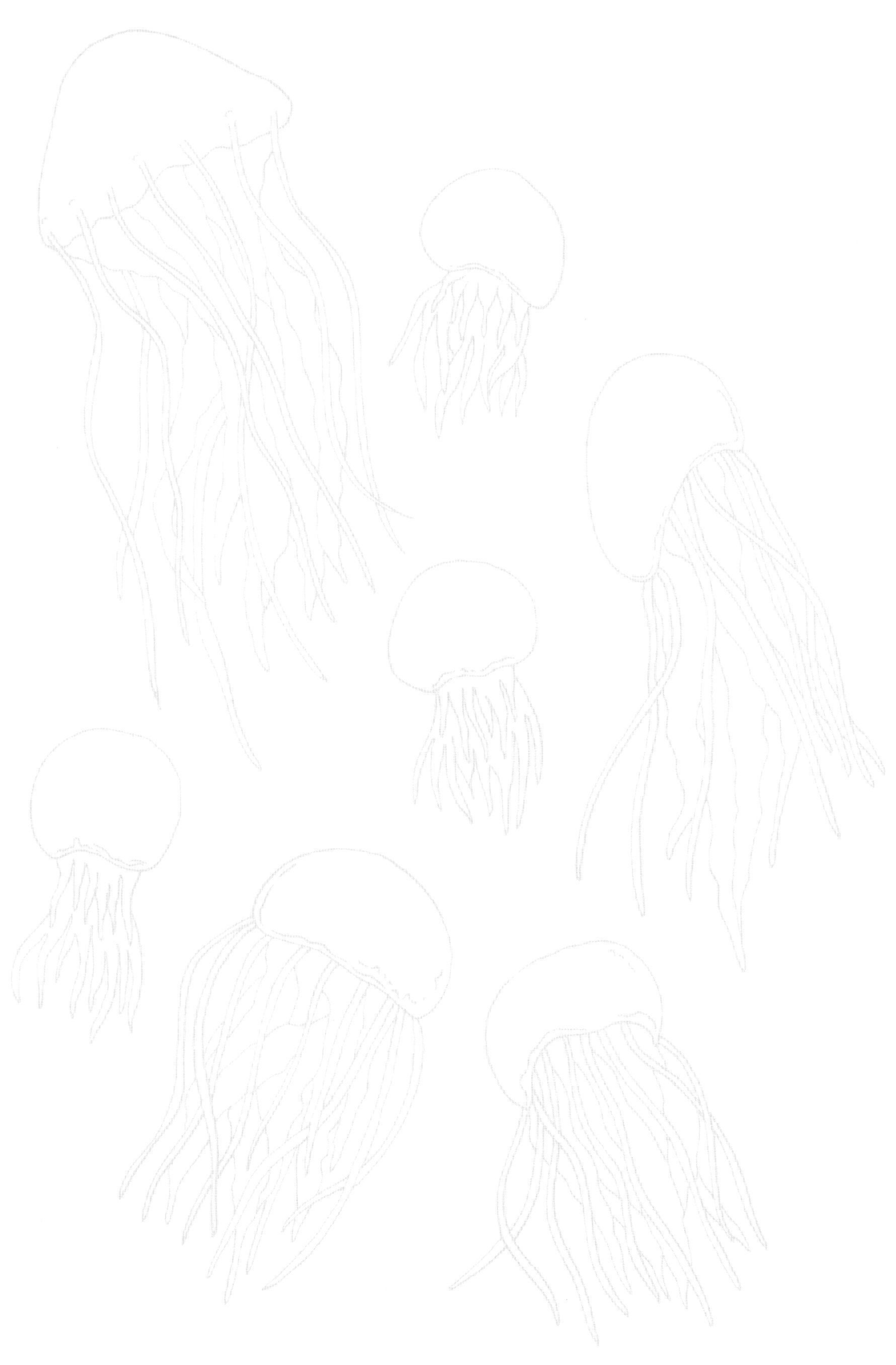

 LAYERING SINGLE COLOURS
Working in a monochrome palette (page 13). Mix the colours together to create additional shades
that complement each other.

DELIBERATE BLEEDING
Practise working wet-on-wet (page 15). Leave the paint to dry fully before adding the black watermelon seeds, so the black doesn't run into the red.

 REALISTIC RUNS
Practise incorporating drips (page 19). Create the drips with a really wet paintbrush. Keep adding water to the same area and hold the page upright to encourage it to run.

 SOFT GLAZING
Practise wet-on-wet glazing techniques (page 20). To remove harsh edges where the paint has
dried, gently rub the area with a wet paint brush.

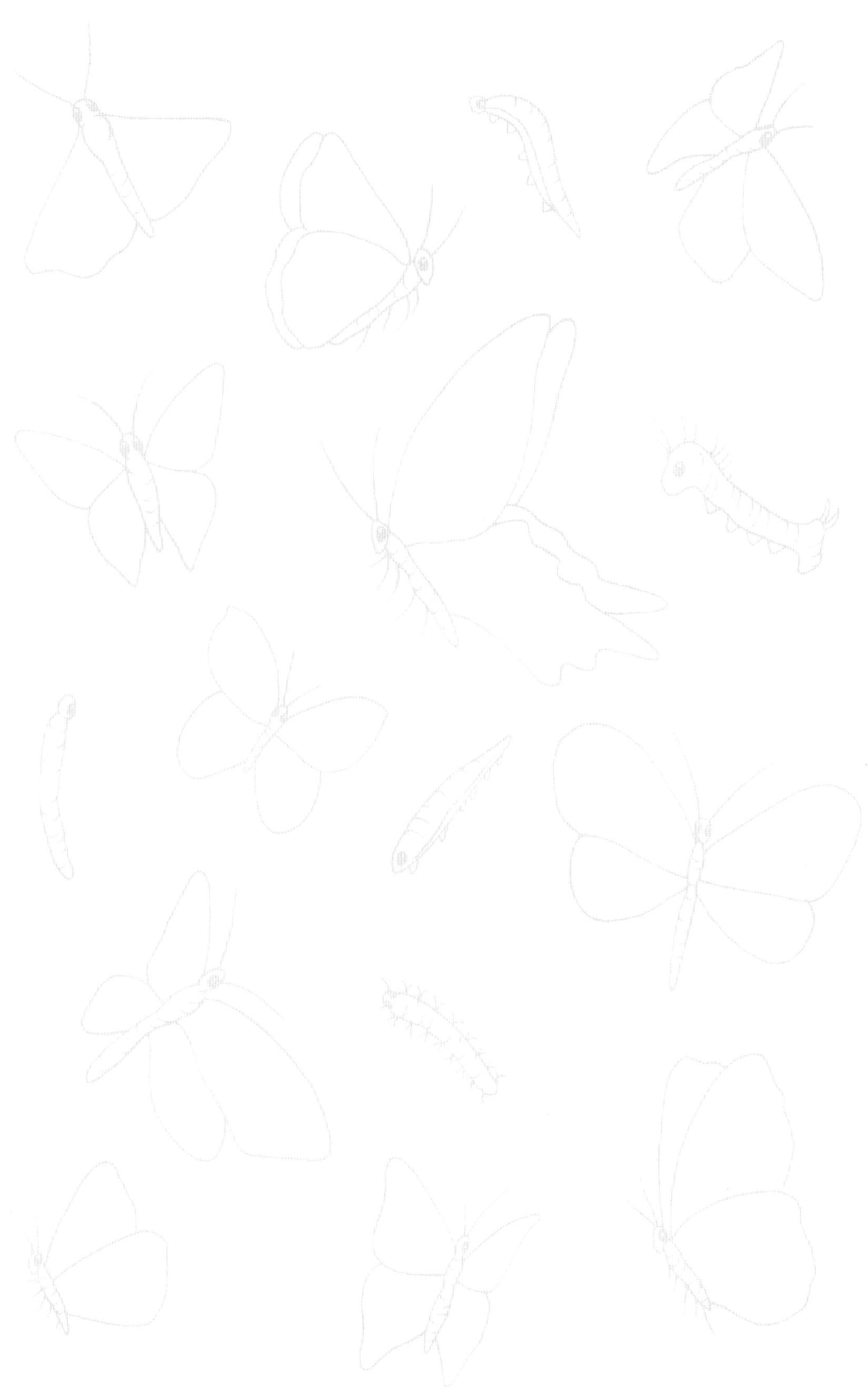

LAYERING FOR BOLD COLOUR

Practise wet-on-dry glazing techniques (page 21). Apply the blocks of paint alongside each other to keep the colours strong. Overlap the colours to produce extra shades.

 GLAZING WITH FEW COLOURS
Practise monochrome glazing (page 21). Allow each layer to dry fully so that the patterns in the fish scales are bold.

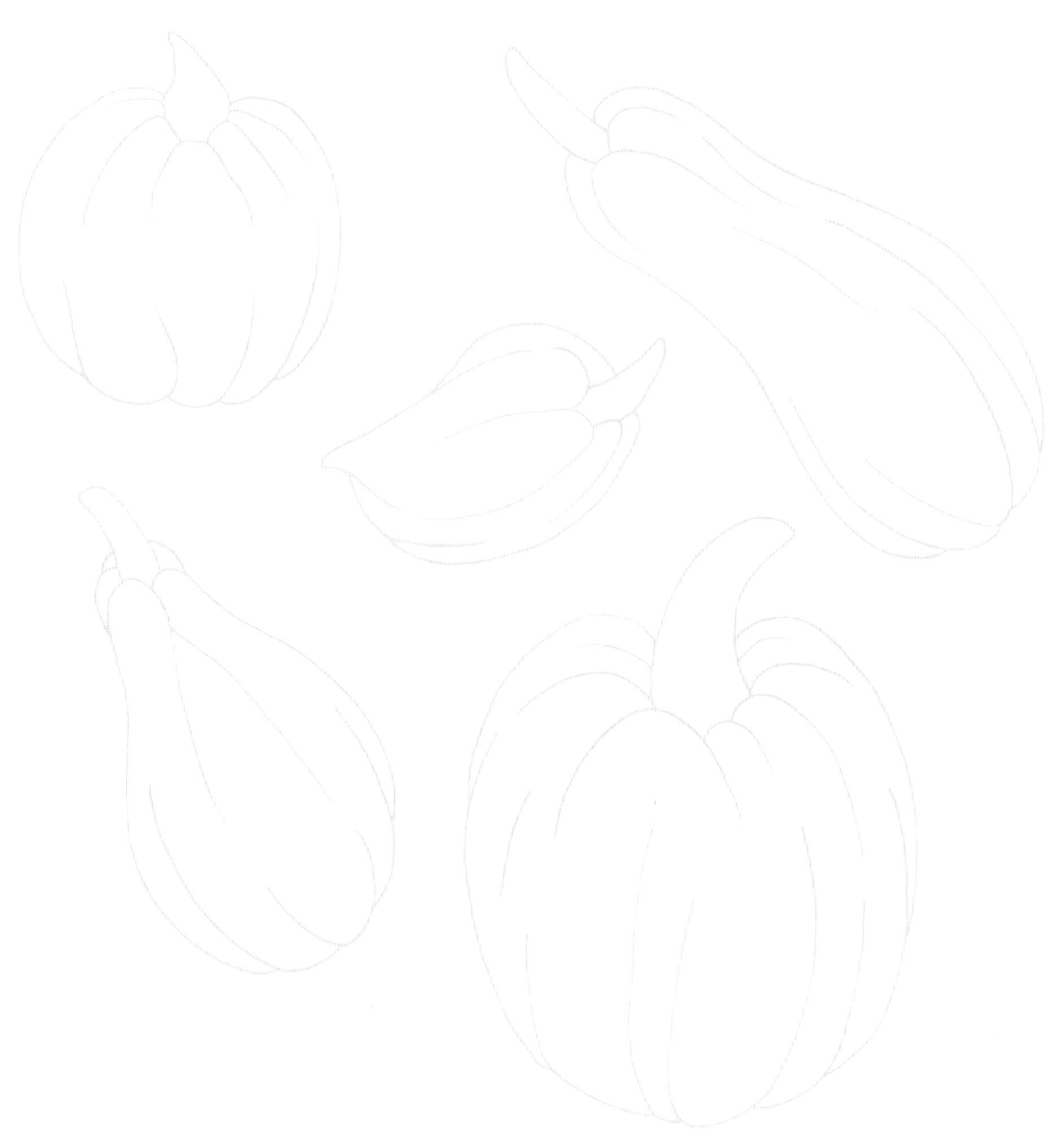

CREATING SHAPE AND TEXTURE
Practise pulling colour (page 23). Add a burst of an alternative colour such as green or yellow, so that your gourds are striking.

 LIGHT AS REFLECTIONS
Working with paper highlights (page 25). Use the same paint colour and add varying amounts of
water to create multiple shades and reflections.

 HIRAMEKI
Practise drawing what you see (page 26). Relax your hand while creating your paint splodges in order to make them more natural and less uniform.

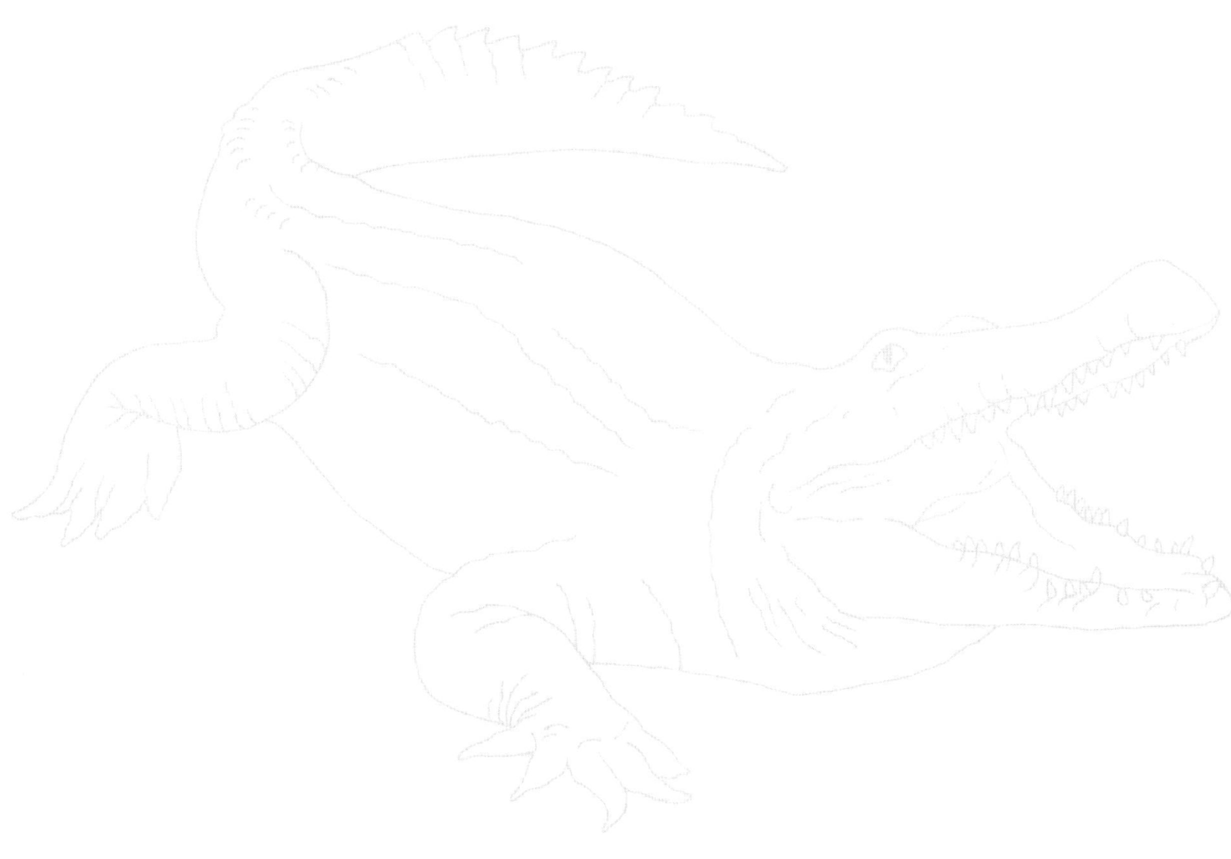

38 **SPONGE WORK**
Practise creating texture (page 29). Leave each sponged layer to dry before applying the next to create more texture.

40 **COLOUR PENCILS**
Practise using watercolours with colour pencils (page 30). Finish by adding small textures with colouring pencils once the paint has dried.

 PEN
Practise adding fine details with pen (page 31). Adding pen before painting will soften the darkness
of the ink. Adding pen afterwards will make a bolder outline.

 SUCCULENTS
Practise the repeating patterns of succulents (page 35). Before each layer fully dries, add the next
so that the different shades of green blend softly together.

 FAIRYTALE MUSHROOMS
Practise adding fine details with pencil and pen (page 35). Try to learn when to stop adding
too much detail before it gets overworked.

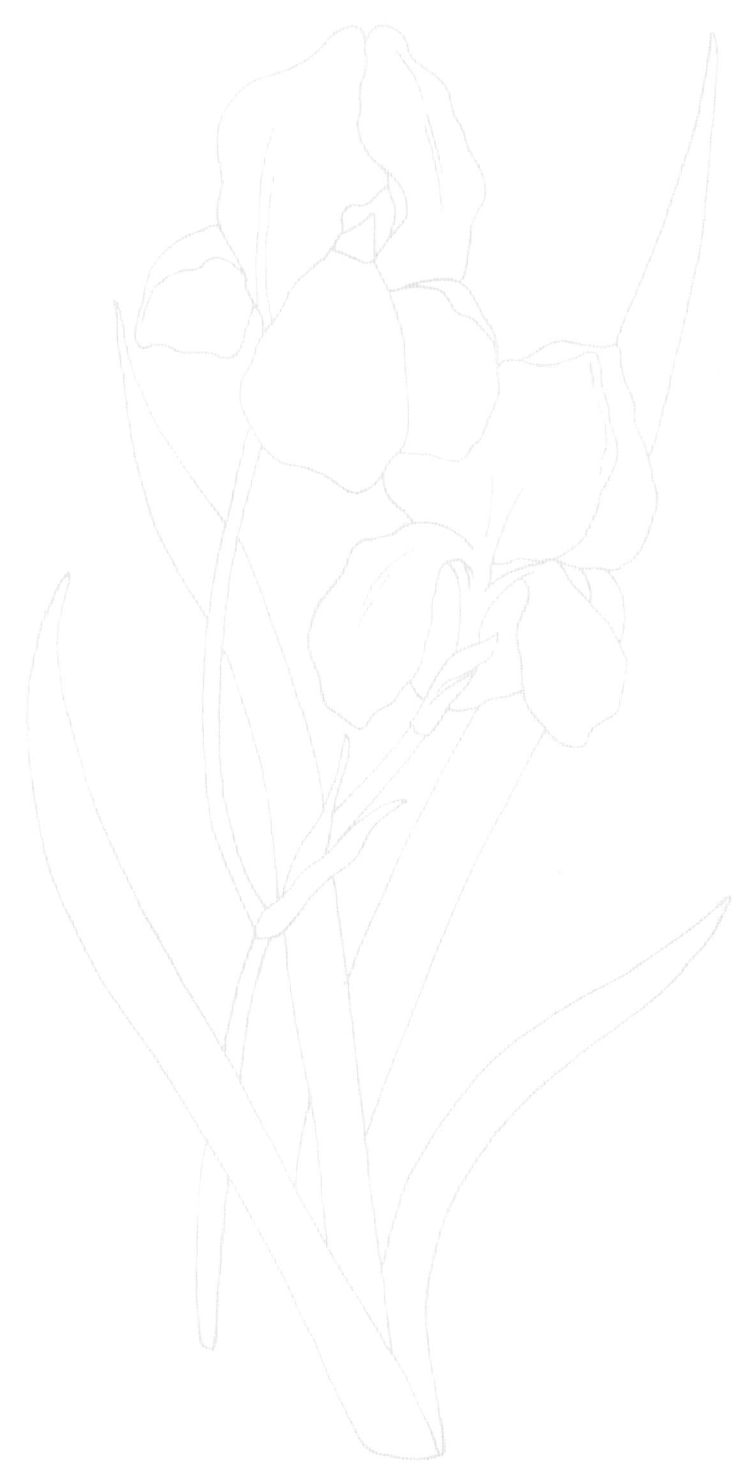

51 DETAILED FLOWERS
Practise combining techniques to create a botanical painting (page 37). Use different shades of the same colour by adjusting the amount of water on the brush.

54 **ANIMAL REALISM**
Practise your pen work to add fine details (page 39). Use a mixture of soft glazing to shape the body and bold wet-on-dry touches for the thinner body parts.

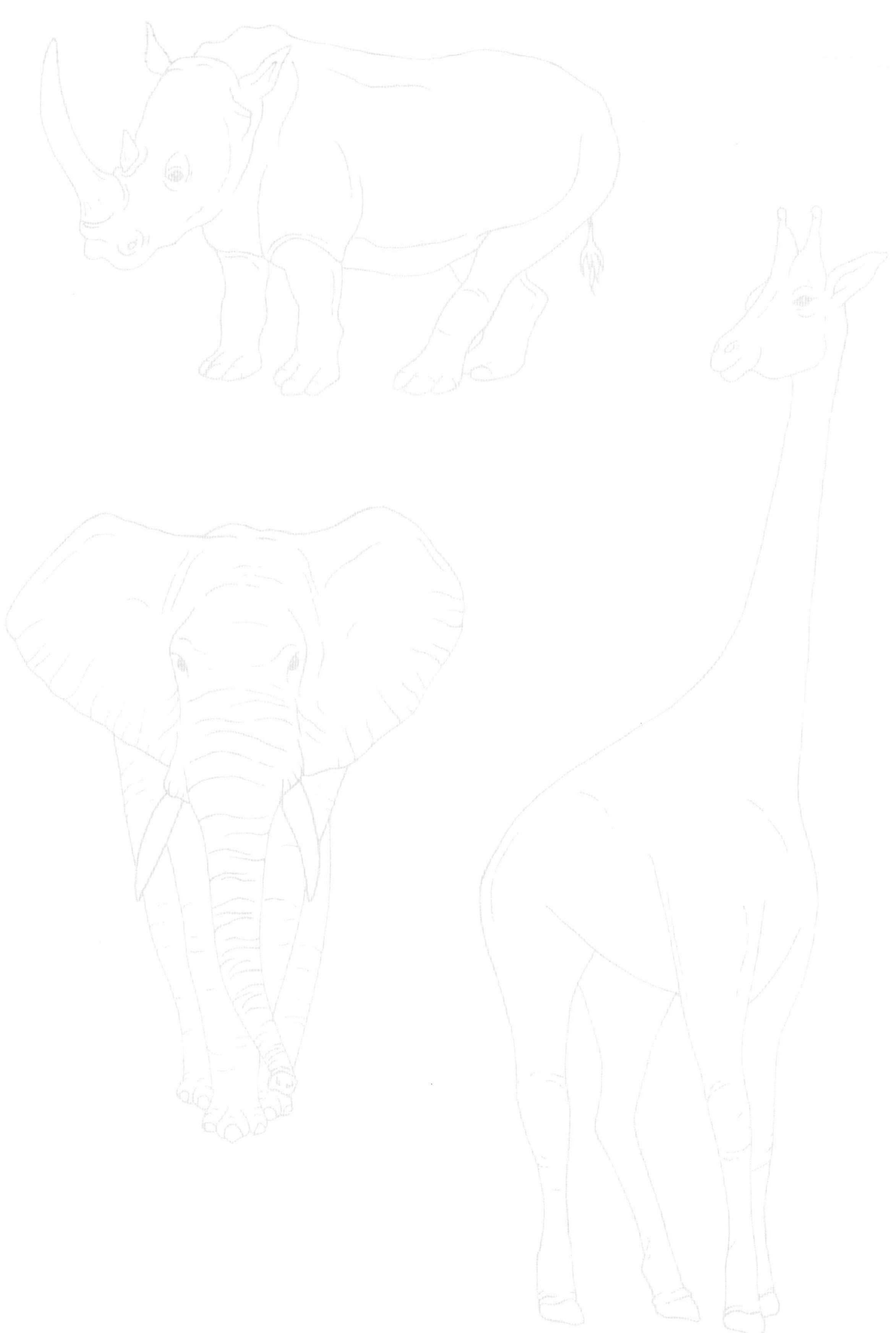

 SKIN AND HIDE
Practise creating realistic animal skins (page 39). Alter the shape of the giraffe's spots to show the
animal's form and create volume.

 PACKAGING
Practise creating highlights (page 40). Apply a light base wash first, which will eventually become your highlight. The lighter this layer, the bolder your highlights will be.

57 BAKED GOODS
Practise creating texture with darker shades (page 41). Leave brushmarks and textures to create the crumbly cookie effect.

 WHAT'S ON YOUR PLATE?
Practise painting various food textures (page 41). Use blocks of colours for your burger fillings,
and keep the glazing to the bun to make it pop!

 CROPPING

Practise creating a swatch of colours before you start (page 42). Create your guidelines with pencil or a very light wash of paint. These lines will be covered as your layers build up.